Doing business in China online

The most comprehensive guide to digital marketing in China

Val Kaplan

Table of contents

Preface

The information in this book reflects the state of Chinese marketing as of the end of 2016. Keep in mind however, that things are changing fairly fast in China and the tools and techniques discussed in this book may not stay optimal or effective in a few years or even a few month from now. In order to stay informed and keep your business strategy up to date, please visit my blog at (sampi.co/blog) on a regular basis.

Why online marketing in China is the key

In light of the early 2016 Chinese stock market fall, sudden devaluation of yuan, manufacturing slowdown and talks about troubled real estate market there are signs of growing concern for a long term prospects of Chinese economy. News reports regularly warn us about upcoming Chinese economic crash with predictions of all sorts of doom and gloom. I would argue that the long term prospect for Chinese economy still looks fairly bright which, if nothing else, could be entirely driven by the rise of Chinese middle class.

Incidentally, these people also represent a new type of consumer – the one who gets most of the information online, reasonably receptive to clever advertisement, active in social media and, ultimately, buying products and services online.

When it comes to Chinese economy, the strongest argument in favor of it continuing to grow and develop is the enormous potential of local consumption. This, in turn, is driven by the rise of Chinese middle class that is becoming both larger and more sophisticated. This development presents unmatched opportunities for foreign companies to sell their products and services to the rapidly growing pool of potential buyers online.

Throughput the history, foreign traders were often frustrated with China, mainly because the majority was just too poor to afford Western products. This is no longer the case.

This chart from the Economist shows that the Chinese middle class is predicted to increase tenfold in 10 years from 2010 to 2020 to 472 million (the middle class is defined here as a household with enough money to buy a car, a TV, a fridge and a smartphone.):

Prosperity ahead

China's middle class, % of households

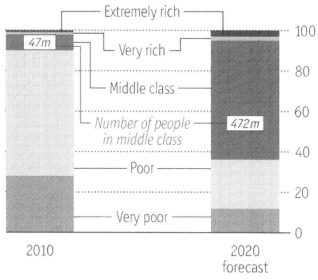

Sources: McKinsey & Company; *The Economist*

Chinese consumer is also becoming more sophisticated and discerning which leads to intensified competition. Investment in proper marketing in China is becoming increasingly important as it also differs quite a bit from what foreign companies could expect in their home markets.

Essentially, this is what this book is all about – how foreign companies can adapt their existing marketing practices to Chinese market and devise new effective marketing strategies that deliver real results.

In this book I focus primarily on online digital marketing for two reasons. First, practice proves that it is the most efficient and cost effective channel in China and it is becoming increasingly so. It is also widely predicted that digital aspect of marketing will inevitably become the most important element in overall marketing strategy as people will continue moving more of their traditionally offline activity into online realm.

In addition, in China, people tend to distrust traditional media, such as TV, radio or print because it is more often associated with "the official line", something that is not always trustworthy. This makes relatively novel channels, such as social or mobile media to be perceived as a source of more reliable information.

The second reason is the unprecedented proliferation of ecommerce in China. Chinese ecommerce market is already larger than that of US and is predicted to pass $1 trillion mark in 2019.

This makes digital marketing a natural choice for promoting anything that can also be bought online, which, in China's case, is pretty much everything. The ability to place a point of sale just a click away from an ad shortens the sales cycle and makes conversions much faster and easier to achieve. Compare it with the traditional case of TV advertisement for a cheeseburger which you are forced to watch while you are not even hungry for one. The next time, when you are actually want to get a cheeseburger, you probably wouldn't even remember anything about the excellent deal you saw on TV.

Of course, traditional ads still work but for them to be efficient, the massage must be constantly repeated to achieve what is often called "frequency" in marketing and this is why TV ads are so expensive.

Another two added advantages of digital marketing that are not specific to China are the ability to target much narrower audience and reliable measurements of a marketing campaign efficiency. This type of measurement, often called analytics, allows advertiser to get a snapshot of everything that is going on with the campaign in real time, compare it with other campaigns running simultaneously or against past benchmarks. The changes and fine tuning can be done almost instantly, allowing constant tweaking of various parameters in order to get better results.

Let us turn to the details next.

How to research competition with Baidu, ecommerce sites and social media

Every proper marketing campaign in any market should first start with market research. Fortunately, it doesn't always have to be an expensive market study, complete with complex competitive analysis and forecasts.

Often times, a simple internet research would do just fine, but, of course, you should first know where and how to look.

Here is the outline of what channels would be able to provide information fast and cheap and, at the very least, would give you a glimpse of what is out there.

It is also worth noting that almost all the tools that I describe in this book require some knowledge of Chinese language as they are not available in English version. On top of that, any research would require searching for the terms in Chinese as well. This basically means that, unless you are fluent in Mandarin, you would need to get some help.

At the end of this book, there are some useful links to resources where you can get that help in case you need it.

Baidu searches

Due to number of reasons, the familiar digital marketing tools, which are mainly run by Google in the Western markets, are not available in China. Google search engine market share in China has fallen below 1% this year and all of other Google services, such as Google docs, Google maps, Google analytics etc., have also become blocked from access. This fact alone is making life quite difficult not only for marketers but for regular citizens and businesses.

Luckily, there is an alternative and it is Baidu (baidu.com), the largest Chinese search engine with about 60% market share.

In fact, just a few years ago, Baidu was much more dominant reaching about 80% of the total search market. Since then, other popular services became more competitive and managed to grab larger market share away from Baidu. Those platforms are 360 Search (haosou.com) and Sogou (sogou.com) holding somewhere around 30% and 15% respectively as of the end 2014.

Here I will be mainly focusing on Baidu however, all the other search engines are fairly similar and can also be used for the purpose of basic market research.

Just like with Google, your basic research can start with a simple search term of a product translated to Chinese.

Now, a word of caution – I strongly advise against using Google Translate or other machine translation program for that. You must find a native speaker to verify the term that you are interested in.

Let me give you an example. Suppose you are interested to search for the keyword "sunglasses". Here is what Google Translate would return:

Unfortunately, even though the translation may technically be correct, no one in China actually uses the term 太阳镜.

The proper term for sunglasses is 太阳眼镜 and this is what you should be using for Baidu search. Once again, Google Translate cannot be relied upon even for a translation of simple keywords, let alone complex "long tail" ones.

Anatomy of a typical Baidu search results

Here is an example of a Baidu search results for the term "sunglasses" (太阳眼镜). Paid results are typically grouped at the top and on the right panels like in the example below:

Compared to a typical Google search results page, with Baidu, it is somewhat harder to tell the difference between paid and organic results. In fact, the only thing that indicates paid ads would be a small word "推广" at the bottom right.

For popular keywords, there would be very few organic results (if any at all) on the first results page. This however is going to change soon once Baidu implements new government sponsored guidelines that require paid ads not to exceed 30% of the total search results page's "real estate".

Next, you would typically see results from Baidu-owned sites like Baike (equivalent to Wikipedia) or Baidu Zhidao (Chinese "Yahoo answers").

News related results would be ranked next, followed by the results from ecommerce sites. Interestingly enough, links to the largest ecommerce platforms belonging to another Chinese tech giant Alibaba, Taobao and Tmall, would not be displayed at all. This is the result of the fierce competition between Baidu and Alibaba.

Finally, closer to the end of the page in this example, you can finally see some organic results followed by another block of ads.

What can you learn from Baidu search? First, you can immediately see the level of competition in your intended market. If there are many paid ads, be prepared to compete with those advertisers for the same keywords.

Next, you will be able to learn who the main competitors are and what they are offering. It is a good idea to visit their sites, explore their offers and get an impression of their sales strategies and distribution channels.

Finally, basic search would give you a better sense on whether it would be wise to invest in Baidu pay-per-click (PPC) or SEO to get ranked organically. I'm going to discuss those choices in more details in the later section.

Marketplace sites search

If you are selling a physical product, one of the best ways to find out what is already available is to research Taobao (Taobao.com), the primary C2C marketplace in China and its B2C equivalent, Tmall (tmall.com).

Both platforms belong to Alibaba and are similar to Amazon, although much bigger.

As mentioned before, none of Taobao or Tmall results will appear in Baidu searches, this is why it is important to research this channel separately.

While typing the search term ("sunglasses" in our example), more results will be shown as you type in, giving some insights on what other terms are frequently searched for (of course, you need to understand Chinese to make sense of it):

Additional search terms may give you some more clues on what else you should be researching.

Taobao will also display a multilevel filters enabling more targeted searches. In case of "sunglasses", the results can be filtered by glasses shapes (oval, round, square, aviator, rectangular etc.), lens color, suitability for different type of face, gender and so on, as well as price range.

The results, each with an attractive product photo, short description and the price, will be displayed right below the filters:

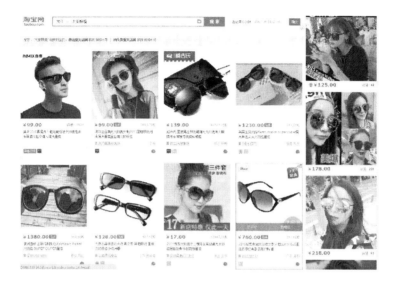

Typically, most results will be linking to either Tmall (like in the case of branded products) or Taobao itself.

What the difference between Taobao and Tmall? Tmall is a type of an upscale version of Taobao with a strict policy against fakes. In the physical world, Tmall can compared to a branded department store while Taobao is more of a bazaar style market.

How Taobao can help you with the market research? First of all, it is the best channel for researching product prices and price ranges for different subcategories of products.

Secondly, you will be able to better understand the overall popularity of the product category, competition and sales channels.

Finally, seeing so many competing offers grouped together may give you more insight on how yours could fit in the mix.

Side note: occasionally, you may even find your own products sold by someone else that you may not be aware of!

One of the most popular features that was recently introduced by Chinese main ecommerce sites is the option to search using an image or an actual product photo. User simply uploads the image of a product to Taobao website or a mobile app and the site will return most closely matched results. This functionality can work surprisingly well for some easily identifiable products but may not be perfectly suited for others. In any case, it is another tool that can be employed for marketing research purpose.

Social media

The third channel that I recommend for basic market research is the social media. In China, Sina Weibo and WeChat are the two most popular platforms. Sina Weibo has evolved around desktop use while WeChat works with mobile. I'm going to discuss those platforms in much more details in the subsequent sections of this book. For now, suffice it to say that, for the purpose of market research, Weibo is much more suitable and this is what I will be focusing on next.

First of all, searching for something like "sunglasses" on Weibo is unlikely to be a very useful exercise – most results would probably be quite irrelevant returning mostly news or pictures of people wearing sunglasses.

It is much better to conduct more focused searches such as using specific brand names of competitors for example.

In any case, when it comes to searches for social mentions, Weibo is fairly similar to Twitter with the difference that instead of preceding a term with #, it should be enclosed with # like this: #太阳眼镜#.

One useful aspect of a search for a broad term is finding out who is advertising with that keyword. Here is the screenshot of a sample search results with the ads shown on the lower right panel:

The best way to use social media search is to find out about the competition and how they are using this channel. For example, let's search for one of the most famous brands of sunglasses – Oakley (the brand name search doesn't require #):

The first result would usually be the official brand account followed by news and social mentions which also can be quite useful.

While browsing competitors' accounts it is a good idea to note how many followers they have, their posting frequency and whether they are engaging followers in their tweets.

In the above example, Oakley's account reveals a fairly active channel with over 80K followers and 5.5K tweets (as of Oct 2015). The company seems to be engaging in promotions via sponsored sports events and many tweets feature new designs and product launches:

In summary, social media searches on Weibo are best for researching competitors and their ways of using this highly effective marketing channel. It can help you to figure out how much emphasis on social media your marketing campaign should be placing and what you should be tweeting about in order to maximize engagement with your targeted audience.

Chinese website localization: translation, design, payment systems, SEO, live support

Having a localized website for Chinese market is one of the essential steps a foreign company should undertake in order to build trust and improve brand awareness locally. Localization is not the same as translation of the content, although translation is the major part of it. My own experience suggests that it isn't a quick process and, most importantly, it requires careful planning and verifying every step with your contractor. We are turning to this part next.

Translation

Investing in a qualified translation of a website can hardly be underestimated. Poorly translated site is not only an off-putting one to visitors, it also gives an impression that the product or service behind it is probably just as poor.

When it comes to Chinese market, it is often a good idea to have your site translated to both Simplified Chinese for

Mainland audience and to Traditional Chinese used in Hong Kong and Taiwan.

Even though, both Taiwanese and Hongkongese would have little problem reading content in Simplified Chinese, having those two choices would be seen as showing respect to millions of Traditional Chinese readers. Large number of corporate executives and managers of companies in China are from Taiwan and Hong Kong and, depending on your industry, it would certainly help offering them proper translation as well.

If you are on a bootstrap budget, the first thing to try would be finding a freelance translator through sites like Elance.com or Odesk.com (recently merged into Upwork.com). It is by far the cheapest option but could also be a hit and miss.

Many freelance translators, who are native Chinese speakers, don't have a good grasp of Traditional Chinese and would simply use machine translation program, like Google Translate, that simply substitutes Simplified characters with Traditional ones. As a result, Traditional Chinese translation would look awkward and, sometimes, completely unreadable. If you use any of the freelance translators, make sure to test them first by asking them to translate a paragraph to both languages and have it verified with a native Taiwanese or Hongkongese.

A word of caution: never hire translators who are not native Chinese speakers, this would be a complete waste of your money. You should also make sure to verify the work before you release the payment.

If your company is lucky enough to have a decent budget for a website translation, then, by all means, consider a professional translation firm or a local marketing localization agency. They would typically pay more attention to details that lie beyond a straightforward translation, such as proper formatting of time, date and currency.

You still have to exercise caution while hiring a professional translation company – unfortunately, many of them are simple one-two man operations, regardless of what they say about themselves on their website. Moreover, large number of them would also use machine translation software with some corrections afterwards. Be prepared to shop around for a while because, in my experience, 80% of such small firms do not offer high quality work.

Just like with the freelancers, you should test the quality of translation first by asking them to translate one paragraph.

If you suspect that machine translation has been used for any of the languages (most likely Traditional Chinese), do not hire them.

If you are prepared to spend anywhere around $1,000 or more, make sure to have a written contract with such company. The contract should stipulate that the company must correct the translation within 2-4 weeks after submitting it to you in case any issues are detected later on. There must be a legal recourse clause in the contract in case of substandard quality of the translation but it is always time limited, so make sure to check their work carefully as soon as you receive it.

Now to the technical side. Most websites use CMS (content management system) that make inserting new language a much easier process than editing HTML or XML files. You have to make sure that your system supports Chinese which shouldn't be a problem with all modern CMS.

A website can also be configured to load a specific language based on IP address location. However, there should be an option to change an automatically selected language because not everyone who may visit your site should be assumed to be able to read Chinese. Besides, IP address based geolocation would not work if a site visitor uses VPN – the most common way to bypass China's infamous Great Firewall to get access to blocked sites.

Design

There is an ongoing debate on whether it is a good idea to completely redesign a website for Chinese market or reuse the same styling of the original main site. Some companies believe that consistency of the brand image across different countries and cultures is more important. Another view suggests that adopting to local tastes and preferences is the right approach.

If you have spent some time looking at Chinese ecommerce websites, you can't help but notice how incredibly cluttered they look. In fact, most of that apparent clutter is a result of link-heavy nature of Chinese internet in general.

What might strike a Westerner as an overwhelming overload of information is likely to be perceived as a content rich and intuitive site by the Chinese.

Here is an example of the most popular Chinese ecommerce site, Taobao.com:

And this is a screenshot of Ebay.com which is the closest equivalent to Taobao in the West:

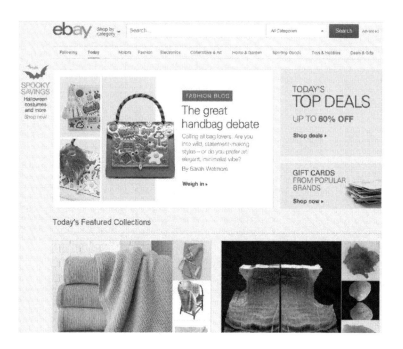

Clearly, there is a major difference between the two: Ebay uses modern clean design with lots of white space while Taobao seems old fashioned and too cluttered. On the other hand, Taobao is still making much more money with their not-so-pretty looking platform than Ebay with their nice and sleek one.

The bottom line is that, while deciding on the most effective visual design solution for a website, you should put your own personal esthetic preferences aside and focus on what best works for the Chinese market that you are targeting.

There are couple of explanations of why Chinese still prefer "cluttered" designs as opposed to "clean" ones. First one that I came across was given by Yu Gang and David Wei in their interview with CNN correspondent Kristie Lu Stout in one of CNN episodes "On China":

"Our consumers like a page very crowded, busy with lots of links, at the same time you opening many windows at the same time... So when you go into the Chinese consumer psyche, they want to have a chaotic bazaar type experience...They want to create this shopping atmosphere"

Another explanation on what is behind the preference towards link heavy sites in China was given by Barry Lloyd's, President of WebCertain Asia:

"There is one reason in particular that mainland Chinese sites are incredibly link heavy, and that is that people tend to forget that full literacy in China is a relatively recent development and, when combined with the internet which also uses a "foreign" alphabet, there can be real issues of confidence when people are typing in things to their browser window or when searching through uncertainties with their spelling. This, in turn, has a huge impact on how people navigate to different sites and pages within a site.

This is not to say that the Chinese are bad readers. Far from it! But Simplified Chinese, which enabled the whole country to be able to read and write, was only really started as a process in 1952 and became introduced over the next 2 decades to become the form it is currently in – developing throughout this period. Officially, it is still under development and a series of further changes were put forward in 1977 but not generally taken up, and even as recently as 2009 public discussions were started on changing the language further – so no wonder people are confused on how to spell things!

Outside of mainland China (apart from Singapore), all other Chinese enclaves still use Traditional Chinese and in conversations these people make comparisons in that Simplified Chinese being established as a written language is similar to English speakers being told to read and write in the sort of short-hand used nowadays by people texting on their phones. "

There are few additional points that have to be considered while localizing a site for China. First, Chinese translation of an English equivalent will always be shorter, making paragraphs smaller. This may affect overall look of the sites as some visual elements may shift or not displayed exactly as intended. Usually, minor styling tweaks would be enough to fix that.

Second, it is a good idea having another look at the images in order to make sure that they are culturally appropriate and are just as appealing to a Chinese viewer as they are to a Westerner. The best way to do that is to show design prototypes to native Chinese, preferably within the intended target group, to get firsthand opinion on how they feel about website's visual style and imagery.

Loading optimization

Loading speed is one of the most important metrics of a website performance and is directly linked to bounce rate (the percentage of visitors who enter the site and then leave rather than continuing on to view other pages within the same site) and search engine ranking. Typically, if it takes more than 5 seconds to load a page, a visitor would be more likely to move on. Loading time within 2 seconds is considered to be the optimal case.

Not surprisingly, loading time is also a major factor in website ranking with search engines like Google or, in China's case Baidu.

Unfortunately, even if your website is loading fast in your main market such as US or Europe, it is almost certain that it will be slower in China. There are two main reasons for it: websites that are physically hosted outside of China have to pass the "Great Chinese Firewall" – a set of censorship methods set up by Chinese authorities and designed to restrict internet access to websites hosted on foreign servers. The process slows down data transfers and, ultimately, affects the loading speed of foreign based websites.

Obviously, the easiest way to circumvent this problem would be to setup hosting in China but, presently, this requires ICP (Internet Content Provider) license, a permit issued by the Chinese Ministry of Industry and Information Technology that allows China-based websites to operate within the country. ICP license can only be obtained by a Chinese registered business (with some very rare exceptions), which means that incorporating a company in China would be a pre-requisite.

Payment systems

Chinese online payment systems market is already a remarkably well developed industry, especially considering its relatively late start. With ecommerce annual growth rate at around 20%, Chinese online payment systems serve as one of the most important technological enabler.

Chinese online shoppers also grew to trust online payments and the vast majority is quite comfortable using it to pay for purchases on the internet. Alipay, the most popular Chinese online payment system by Alibaba, holds the largest market share. It powers two largest ecommerce platforms, Taobao and Tmall and is extensively used in large number of third party applications and platforms.

As of the end of 2015, Alipay accounted for almost 70% of the entire Chinese online payment market. It is fair to say that almost everyone in China with a cellphone and a bank account has Alipay account which is somewhere around 700 million people.

In addition, Alipay doesn't charge any fees for local transactions with the exception of withdrawing large amounts back to traditional bank accounts. In general, cross border transactions are not free and the fee structure depends on the type of contract a merchant has with Alipay as well as the transactional volume.

The second largest online payment system is TenPay developed by Tencent. In fact, TenPay also powers WeChat Pay, the payment system used by WeChat users. Thanks to this app's explosive growth, TenPay was able to increase its market share quite significantly during 2015 to about 20%, primarily on the account of Alipay.

WeChat Pay is now extensively used for many types of transactions. With web payments, customers simply scan the QR Code with their mobile phones directly from WeChat app in order make a payment to a website. For mobile users, WeChat Pay is used for payment within WeChat Official Accounts to enable sales from within the app.

Both Alipay and WeChat Pay are increasingly used for offline transactions at traditional stores and restaurants in China and even abroad. A customer simply opens the app in order to allow the merchant to scan their QR code with a special scanner or, often, just another smartphone. As many phones now have fingerprint scanning sensor, placing a finger on it is all it takes to complete the transaction (otherwise, a customer has to type in a secret code in the app). Alternatively, a customer can simply scan a merchant's QR code to send the payment.

Since those type of transactions are free to customers, Alipay and WeChat Pay serve as substitutes for carrying cash or credit cards and offer both security and convenience.

Alipay and TenPay (WeChat Pay) account for almost 90% of current mobile payment while other players, such as Lakala, JD wallet, YeePay, 99Bill and others are still quite far behind.

As for foreign alternatives, PayPal was not able to get any meaningful user base so far and is unlikely to do so in the future. Apple Pay still barely registers in China mobile payment market, although it is still quite new.

SEO

Search Engine Optimization (SEO) is the essential process that every website should go through at the beginning as well as throughput its existence. Optimizing a website for main keywords ensures that it will be found with Chinese search engines, such as Baidu, Sogou, Qihoo etc.

There are basically two ways to go about SEO: do it yourself or outsource to professionals. Someone who is technical and understands the SEO basics, may be quite capable to perform onsite part of the process. However, the offsite component of SEO which mainly involves link building with other sites, is a long and fairly time consuming process. It would also involve detailed knowledge of Chinese internet, building relationship with relevant sites, submitting and syndicating content to popular blogs and directories as well as social media component.

Reputable SEO companies would typically have such process already setup and most likely be more successful in offsite part of SEO. On the other hand, hiring SEO services from specialized providers can be quite expensive.

In some cases, an in-depth look into cost vs. potential benefits of SEO is needed in order to determine whether this is a worthwhile investment.

On the other hand, onsite SEO, at least in its basic form, is something that should be done in every case. Most importantly, website developer should be aware of certain quirks of Baidu and make certain adjustments early on. Getting it right from the beginning will at least make it possible for your Chinese website to rank high with the main search engines. Get it wrong and your website may not show up high enough in searches to be found or, worse, will never be indexed by Baidu.

Here are 10 most important aspects to keep in mind in relation to optimizing a website for Baidu:

#1: Subdomains or multiple domains

Baidu generally dislikes subdomains – a very common structure of multilingual websites. For example, you should avoid setting up en.mysite.com for English and zh.mysite.com for Chinese. Baidu prefers to have different languages on completely separate domains. For example, if www.mysite.com is your main site, www.mysite.cn could be its Chinese language equivalent. Admittedly, this arrangement is harder to maintain, however, if you want to rank high on Baidu – do not use subdomains.

#2: Using robot.txt file

Another Baidu quirk is disfavoring robot.txt file – Google's standard way to communicate with search engine crawlers. This is the most common way to tell search engines which pages should not be crawled. For the purpose of your China web presence, those specific instructions should be set in .htaccess file or in server settings and not in robot.txt. This is another reason to use separate domain for your Chinese site (see #1).

#3: Domain names

Baidu ranks .CN country level domains higher than the equivalent .COM and.NET. As .CN domain registration is open to foreigners now, there is no excuse not to grab it. Also, once you have established you China web presence and your brand becomes well-known, chances are that .CN domain may become the target of internet squatters. So, if it is still available, register it early.

#4: Loading time optimization

Long loading time will not only ruin user experience of your Chinese visitors but also lower your Baidu ranking.

The best solution is to host in China, however that requires ICP license issued by Ministry of Industry and Information Technology and is only available to China-registered businesses. Hosting in Hong Kong may improve the loading speed but it still will not be as fast as hosting in China. Signing up with a reliable CDN provider (content delivery network) service, such as CloudFlare, could be another alternative solution.

#5: Broken links to blocked sites

Links to blocked social media sites such as Facebook, Twitter or YouTube will appear broken which will slow down the loading as well (see #4). Also, services like Google fonts wouldn't load at all causing the fonts to look different from the intended set. Google map wouldn't work either and YouTube hosted video wouldn't play. The only solution is to use the local equivalents for blocked services such as Weibo, YouKu and Baidu.

#6: Blacklisted keywords

If your site uses any of the blacklisted keywords, it will be deindexed by Baidu and probably blocked from access too. Wikipedia keeps updated list of blacklisted keywords that are mostly related to politics but keep in mind that the list may change quickly when triggered by specific current events. In any case, staying away from politics in China is probably a good idea anyway.

#7: Keyword research

It is important to do a proper keyword research with the tools available from Baidu rather than Google. Also, the keywords should never be a straight forward translation from English – Google translate or similar tools are absolutely inadequate for this purpose. This is why you should consider seeking help of a professional translator or, at least, run the keywords by a native Chinese speaker.

#8: Using iFrames, JavaScript and Flash

Similar to Google, Baidu can't crawl iFrames and Flash content. Although Google is getting much better in crawling JavaScript, Baidu is still pretty much blind to it. This means that none of your SEO content should be in JavaScript which also includes navigation drop down menu. This is why it is a good practice to have a duplicate footer menu that is not JS based. As for iFrames and Flash – they belong to history anyway.

#9: Link building

At the moment, Baidu still values link quantity over quality, which means that techniques and tricks that used to work with Google 2-3 years ago can still be quite effective for your Chinese website SEO. It is quite likely that, eventually, Baidu will catch up with Google's approach of putting more emphasis on link quality vs. quantity, after all they used to follow Google's every step. In any case, for now, back links from anyone and everything would still bring SEO benefits to your site.

#10: Baidu site submission

Don't count on Baidu finding your site quickly – it is always better to submit it manually. Since, Baidu doesn't have an equivalent to Google webmaster tools, the website has to be re-submitted every time there is a major change using Baidu submission tool.

Live support

One of the most critical components of a successful conversion of Chinese online consumers is live customer service.

Chinese online shoppers have already been spoiled by near instant customer support on major ecommerce sites. For example, large percentage of shoppers on Taobao would often initiate online chat session with a seller before taking a decision to make a purchase.

Regardless of whether it is a product sold from a website or an online service, Chinese visitors would expect to be able to ask questions and get answers within minutes.

Luckily, this can be accomplished in several ways and we are going to look at each of them next.

QQ

QQ messenger is still the most popular chat program in China. Practically every Chinese is familiar with QQ from the early days of the internet. Incorporating QQ into a website is also quite easy – all it takes is pasting a piece of code to your website to display a functional QQ icon.

By clicking a QQ icon, a visitor can start chatting immediately as long as the program is installed on their computer or a mobile device. Fortunately, this is the case for the vast majority of Chinese users anyway.

Toll free number

The good old toll free phone number is the traditional way getting customers to call you directly and it would probably work well if you target somewhat less tech savvy audience.

Toll free numbers in China start with 400 and can be applied for with China's telephone service providers. Typically, they offer several different packages and are fairly inexpensive.

Telephone companies are constantly adding more new features to those numbers such as autoresponders, forward services, voice mails, various types of notifications etc. They also allow to choose a number from an available pool, although the good numbers get picked out quickly. While choosing a 400 number it is best to avoid the "unlucky" digits such as "four". "Eights" and "nines" are the best, so are the repetitive numbers like 55, 66 etc.

WeChat

There are many good reasons to include WeChat contact on the website and using it for live support purpose is just one of them. Once a visitor to a website starts following your company WeChat account, there are many ways to keep them engaged which is a whole separate topic.

Nowadays, increasing number of companies in China choose to provide customer service exclusively through WeChat because it offers much more than just a live chat. For example, WeChat can send pre-programmed answers in response to a specific inquiry with predefined keywords. It can also grab information about users such as their present location and tailor the answers based on that criteria. More advanced companies can even integrate WeChat customer service into a sophisticated CRM (customer relationship management) system that incorporates various types of marketing automation.

One drawback of using WeChat as a customer support channel is the fact that it takes manual scanning of a QR code by a visitor with their cellphone. While this may be convenient for someone visiting from a desktop, browsing site on the mobile device makes that scanning impossible. In this case, a mobile visitor would have to save the QR code as a picture in the photos and then import it to WeChat. Unfortunately, this is not a straight forward process and many people are simply unaware of how to do that.

Live Chat app

Live chat can be integrated with practically any website in a form or a 3rd party plugin. There are many services that offer this type of functionality and they mainly differ in features and price plans. Basic features usually include support for mobile apps, automated responses, alerts and escalation scenarios, various levels of security, ability to share files, routing options etc.

Some of the most popular services that offer Chinese support are Zopim, LiveChat, Zoho Sales IQ as well as many others. Some of them, like Zopim, even offer free plans with limited features set and the prices for paid plans are also fairly affordable in the range of $15-30 per month – well worth the investment.

Search engine marketing in China: available options, Baidu PPC, mobile

Search engine market

China is one of only three major markets where Google is not the dominant search engine. The other two markets are Russia where Yandex holds the commanding market share and Korea with Naver being the most popular choice. In China, Baidu is the largest search engine with market share somewhere between 60% and 75% according to various estimates.

Moreover, Baidu is also the leading choice for searches on mobile devices, the increasingly important Chinese search engines market. In June 2016, it was reported that Baidu had 667 million monthly active users (MAU) just for that month alone.

The entire Chinese search engines market has been growing at fairly steady rate since 2010, adding each year somewhere between 50 and 70 million new users. This year, it is estimated to have reached about 600 million regular users, about three quarters of which go to Baidu as their service of choice.

In many ways, Baidu has been following, if not copying, Google's business strategy. It has diversified its business into areas that are identical to Google's: from navigation and self-driving cars to AI (artificial intelligence) and VR (virtual reality).

Although, it did hit a few bumps on the road, such as recent scandals with its medical ads and illegal promotions of gambling sites, it is hard to imagine Baidu being knocked off its primary position among Chinese search engines any time soon.

The other Chinese search engines that are worth mentioning are Qihoo (aka Search360) and Sogou. Qihoo in particular has been growing relatively fast in recent years and was the only one that was ever in a position to somewhat threaten Baidu's dominance in Chinese search engines market, although it is no longer the case.

When it comes to advertising, Baidu should always be considered as the first choice, mainly because of its largest reach. On average, Baidu CPC (cost per click) tends to be higher than Google across almost all industries. Most likely, it will continue to increase as Baidu has been experiencing fall in profits and will probably continue gradually increasing prices further down the road.

Another reason to focus on Baidu is the fact that its technology is the most advanced. This ultimately affects advertisement CTR (click through rate) through higher relevancy with the search terms.

Baidu has also been active in the video market and currently owns one of the largest online video hosting platforms called iQiYi. As videos are quickly becoming one of the most popular types of content consumed online, Baidu is in a good position to take advantage of that market as well.

In addition, Baidu, like Google, is very good at remarketing which is built into its display network with over 600,000 partner websites in China. Managing both search ads and display ads is done within the same Baidu advertising account where user can simply split the budget between the two channels.

One of the biggest hustles associated with Baidu PPC is opening the advertising account. Unless your company has Chinese business registration, applying for Baidu account involves quite a bit of paperwork and a long verification process. Baidu would typically request translated version of your foreign business license and may require additional proof of incorporation. Companies in financial and medical fields would most certainly be scrutinized more carefully and multiple requests for additional documentation are quite common.

As part of the account registration process, verification of a website (which must be in Chinese) often leads to additional requests to change certain sections, most commonly "about us" part. All this is aimed at making sure that the advertiser is not misrepresenting its business nature and is a legitimate company which will not become involved in promoting anything illegal.

This process is in sharp contrast with Google's where anyone with a Gmail and a credit card can open an account and start running campaigns almost immediately.

The situation is not that much different with other Chinese search engines such as Qihoo and Sogou. They also require business registration and licenses from foreign applicants and must follow similar verification process. Once approved, running PPC campaign with those engines is quite similar to Baidu. On the positive side, for businesses that are not in very competitive niches, CPC on Qihoo and Sogou can be substantially lower compared to Baidu. Therefore, it is a good idea to try those engines as well in parallel, although not instead of Baidu.

Baidu PPC

As long as Baidu remains the largest search engine in China it always should be the first choice for PPC (pay per click) advertising campaign for businesses looking to reach Chinese audience.

In general, the reason PPC marketing can be highly effective is the fact that users who are actively searching for something already have a buying intent. It means that they are more likely to convert, in other words to become the actual customers, compared to those who are passively looking at ads or are still in the process of discovery of a specific product or service.

PPC with Baidu is, in principal, identical to Google's equivalent, although there are several important differences to keep in mind. First of all, due to the fact that Chinese internet is tightly controlled and regulated by the government, opening a PPC account is, by far, more complicated process than with Google.

In contrast to Google AdWords account which is free and only asks for a Gmail account and a credit card, Baidu requires some serious paperwork, a fee and a deposit to get it going.

Currently, only legally registered companies, domestic or foreign, and not individuals, can advertise with Baidu. Obviously, opening Baidu account for a Chinese company is much easier than for a foreign one, it is also cheaper and faster. As mentioned above, overseas business entities are required to provide business registration certificate at the minimum and are often asked to submit additional documentation. This is why it is recommended to enlist a help of professionals who are experienced in dealing with Baidu on behalf of a foreign companies.

Once the account has been registered and activated, it operates in a similar way with Google, although the back-end interface is entirely in Chinese. In addition, the structure is significantly more confusing and takes some time getting used to. Once again, even if you are fluent in Chinese, it is always advisable to outsource Baidu account management to someone who is well familiar with it instead of attempting to do it yourself.

Baidu search ads

On the most basic level, there are two sections in Baidu account: search ads and display ads. Search ads are those that are displayed on search results pages in response to user query. In Baidu, they come in a few different formats.

The most basic format is a text ad complete with a title, two lines of description and URL at the bottom – quite similar to Google. There is also a verification level assigned to an ad which is designed to inform users about trustworthiness of a particular website and an advertiser.

Some text ads can also include additional links to separate landing pages. By offering several options, such arrangement increases likelihood of that ad being clicked, although this format is more expensive.

Baidu brand zone

Baidu Brand Zone is another option that is most suitable for businesses looking to build brand awareness rather than achieve direct conversions. This type of ads typically includes images, text and multiple links. Such ads are CPM (cost per mille/1000 impressions) based and therefore harder to measure. The price for such ads depends on their size and the position, making the advertising in Baidu Brand Zone to be the most expensive type of Baidu marketing.

Using images with Baidu ads

In general, in order to increase CTR (click through rate) advertisers would try to include images in the ads whenever possible as well as pack more links into an ad. Carefully designed text that fits well with dynamic keywords (those that show up in response to the relevant query) is another important factor to consider. This is where A/B split tests come handy and, fortunately, Baidu offers unlimited ways to test and fine tune the best performing combinations.

Another good reason to include images with the ads is the fact that more users, especially on mobile, use pictures to search for products. Baidu's picture matching algorithms continue improving offering more opportunities to display matching ads.

Baidu ads for mobile

Mobile search is another major area of Baidu strength where it holds even larger market share than on desktops. Optimizing ads for mobile involves setting up a call button that dials the number automatically by user simply tapping it from their phones. It works in both mobile browser and Baidu app.

If the business is particularly interested in reaching mobile users, it is worth investing in creating mobile friendly ads with suitable images and shorter, more concise text.

Baidu display ads

Display ads is the second major method to advertise with Baidu. It involves placing image ads (banners) at the most relevant sites that are part of vast Baidu ads display network. This is what is often called remarketing (or retargeting) – the ads are displayed based on a specific user's history of visiting sites or searching for a particular term.

Technically, it is identical to a much larger Google's ads display network, which, like many other things, has been copied by Baidu.

Both search ads and display ads are managed within the same Baidu PPC account sharing advertising budget that can be split between the two methods.

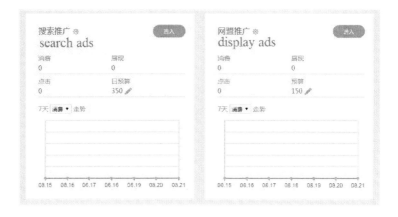

Typically, it is hard to predict in advance which PPC method would bring better results, therefore it should be expected to take some time in order to determine how to best allocate the budget between search and display ads.

PPC vs. SEO

SEO and PPC are the two basic options for boosting traffic to your website. Which strategy is preferable for Chinese market is often a difficult question to answer.

Up until the middle of 2016, Chinese PPC, especially with Baidu, was, on average, delivering better returns than SEO. This was due to several factors:

- First, the search results, especially for popular terms, were dominated by paid ads. In some cases, hardly any organic results would be displayed in the first page;

- Second, there was little visual distinction in Baidu between paid and organic results and most people couldn't even tell the difference.

Things have changed significantly since the most recent scandal involving fraudulent Baidu medical ads that led to the death of young cancer sufferer. Following public outcry and negative publicity, Chinese government published new rules concerning search engine advertising that, among other things, recommended limiting paid results to no more than 30% of SERP (search engine results pages).

Also, the new rules require ads to be more easily distinguishable from organic results in order to minimize the confusion between them.

Baidu, as well as other Chinese search engines, have announced their commitment to comply with the new rules (not that they had any choice in the matter anyway). Less advertising space has inevitably led to increased cost of PPC advertising which has made such campaigns more expensive than they could have been in the past.

On the positive side, the quality of ads is supposed to improve which may, at least in theory, increase public trust in paid ads and improve CTR.

When it comes to SEO, organic results are now guaranteed to feature prominently in Chinese SERPs which makes SEO a more worthwhile investment than it would have been before the new rules were implemented.

On the other hand, you still need to consider different pros and cons of each strategy.

One of the most important consideration is the time frame. Getting results from PPC is almost instant while building SEO traffic takes time. Typically, it would take somewhere between 3 to 6 months to start seeing some benefits from

SEO and 9 to 12 months of consistent efforts to build a stable organic ranking and show up high enough in SERPs. If you can't wait that long than PPC is probably the best route to choose.

In addition, since the feedback is fast and measurable, PPC is best at testing different keywords to see which ones work better. Tweaking SEO keywords takes much longer feedback loop.

Calculating which strategy would be more profitable also requires knowing LTV (life time value) of a customer. This figure can then be compared to the cost of acquiring that customer with either SEO or PPC. As a general rule, SEO tends to be a better fit for high volume, low LTV cases.

Another disadvantage of SEO vs. PPC that is worth mentioning is its sensitivity to Baidu algorithms changes. When that happens, an optimized site can lose ranking practically overnight which makes SEO an ongoing, therefore expensive effort.

Obviously PPC doesn't have this weakness since you are essentially paying Baidu for getting traffic to your site to bypass those ranking algorithms.

On the other hand, organic results are generally considered to be more trustworthy and therefore are more likely to be clicked than the ads. Since now Chinese search engines are required to implement more visual distinction between paid and organic results, visitors are becoming more aware of which is which and tend to favor organic ones.

Considering the above point, SEO seems to offer the better value in search marketing than PPC as a long term strategy. There is an exception however: if your niche is dominated by established players or authority sites that have been building their reputation for years, it is highly unlikely that you would be able to unseat them. However, if you employ PPC you still may be able to outbid them.

In conclusion, choosing between SEO and PPC requires answering three basic questions:

- Can you afford waiting few months for the results or time is of the essence?

- How LTV of your customer stacks against the cost of their acquisition with either strategy?

- How competitive is your space and whether you have a realistic chance to achieve high organic ranking vs. existing sites?

Marketing with Chinese social media: QQ, WeChat, Weibo and others

Ever since world most popular social media platforms, Facebook, Twitter, YouTube and Google+, were blocked in China, the local equivalents have been growing at mind boggling rate. In the last few years, those Chinese social media services have also evolved quite considerably and can no longer be viewed as the "clones" of similar Western platforms.

From marketer's perspective, each Chinese social media platform offers different set of features and possibilities and their value varies quite a bit. I'm going to have a closer look at the most important ones.

QQ and Qzone

Having 850+ million registered accounts, QQ still remains the most popular instant messaging app in China. It was first launched in 1999 by Tencent, the company behind WeChat, and it was initially much like an instant messaging pioneer ICQ, although packed with many more features. Today, QQ messenger offers much more than earlier versions: it has integrated emails, games, music streaming, dating service as well as integration with its social media outlet Qzone.

In fact, every QQ user is also a Qzone member making this platform the biggest in China by the number of subscribers. Unfortunately, despite being an enormous network, QQ and Qzone haven't been able to capitalize on advertising. The main sources of network's revenue are games, sales of digital items and paid membership. Also, arguably, they are in the process of being cannibalized by WeChat, a more innovative service from Tencent.

For advertisers, QQ offers banner placement in the app as well as pop ups but those are quite expensive and, nowadays, largely considered ineffective. The social media outlet connected to QQ messenger, Qzone is divided into different sections. It includes homepage, status, blog, background music, albums, personal information, shared documents, friend visits, friend show, video show, and games. It also allows fairly high degree of profile customization and connectivity to 3rd party applications. Its overall profile design approach is more similar to MySpace rather than Facebook.

Ads in Qzone basically come in 2 varieties: sponsored posts in the user feed and banner ads. After series of page redesigns over the past few years, banners now show up on either left or right side from the feed.

Currently, Qzone for mobile doesn't show any ads and the stress is made on integrating it with QQ messenger while enhancing user experience by adding more options to the core messaging function.

Other methods to market products on Qzone include posting directly in the relevant group discussions as well as commenting. Obviously, this requires maintaining an active presence on the network and making sure that the profile is updated frequently. Luckily, some 3rd party solutions offer cross posting on a number of different platforms, unfortunately, except the most popular – WeChat.

Since Qzone is mostly used by younger audience with limited spending potential it makes it less suitable for promoting large number of categories of products and services. Also, compared to other networks like Sina Weibo, it is more popular in 3rd and 4th tier cities. On the other hand, it still could be an effective route to reach a particular segment such as current or prospective students for example. Companies in educational space, foreign universities looking to attract new students, sellers of hot items popular with teenagers – all can find Qzone an interesting channel to explore.

In the past, Qzone was the venue of choice for a number successful marketing campaigns like XiaoMi, a maker of popular cellphones, or Oreo cookies. Large number of celebrities still maintain active presence on the network, although it is unlikely to be their exclusive channel.

QQ messenger is often used as a direct communication option such as for customer or tech support (see chapter on Live Support). This is why it is often included in websites along with other communication options.

In addition, QQ messenger allows creation of groups (limited to 200 members for basic users and up to 1000 for VIP paid accounts) that can also be leveraged as an effective marketing channel. This feature allows for similar users to be grouped together and engaged all at once.

WeChat

WeChat is the hottest and the fastest growing Chinese social media platform which is entirely mobile based. The first version was released at the beginning of 2011 and has clocked over a billion registered accounts in just about 5 years. In the 3rd quarter of 2016, it has reported 800 million active users 90% of which were in China.

The unprecedented success of WeChat has propelled Tencent, its developer, to become the most valuable tech company in China. Started as a mobile based instant messaging network, WeChat has become much more than that. In fact, today it encompasses the entire ecosystem powered by the platform itself as well as by 3rd party apps.

It is also the most frequently used app in China, installed with over 90% of smartphones. The core functionality of WeChat, which is a two way communication tool, is still the most commonly used feature of the app. However, today, almost anything can be done with just this app alone

– from booking flight tickets and hailing a cab to paying for a meal and sending cash to a friend.

What also makes WeChat unique compared to similar apps like WhatsApp, is its enormous marketing potential. The truth is, however, that WeChat is still trying to balance out the private nature of the network against its capabilities as a marketing tool. This basically means that straight up advertising to users via feed (called "Moments" in WeChat) hasn't really been very popular, although this may change in the future once more innovative targeting methods are introduced.

Presently, the most powerful tool for marketers on this platform is using WeChat official accounts. At the moment, two main types of WeChat official accounts, service and subscription, offer a type of brand marketing channel directed at subscribers who have chosen to follow the channel.

Both service and subscription accounts offer different message display options, although the main differences concern integration with more advanced functionalities.

Subscription account is typically the most basic choice as it is easier to setup and manage. It also allows sending out messages to followers much more frequently – once a day vs. once a week for service account. On the other hand, this type of account does not have any integration options and advanced functionality that can be incorporated into service accounts.

One of the main disadvantages of subscription account is the way the messages are displayed: they will be grouped into one folder containing all the subscription accounts instead of being pushed to user's session list. This means that a follower has to go into that folder to retrieve the delivered content.

Another disadvantage is inability to integrate ecommerce, such as online store. So, if your goal is to enable your users to buy goods online, you should go with the service account.

Generally speaking, if your marketing strategy revolves around pushing content to users, subscription account is just what you need. Verified subscription accounts can also provide some basic customized functionality through a menu. For example, the buttons can be linked to some parts of your website, such as product pages or store locations. In this case, it is highly recommended to have your site optimized for mobile or use responsive design that ensures rendering webpages properly on a small smartphone screen.

On the other hand, if your goal is providing higher degree of functionality to your users through customized menu or offer integrated ecommerce inside the app, verified service account should be the one to consider.

Functionality also differs depending on whether the account has been verified. Currently, only China-registered businesses can have their WeChat account verified. Since foreign based businesses can't open service account as well as verified subscription account, there is just one option available to them – unverified subscription account. Unfortunately, recently this type of account has been stripped of almost any useful functionality including the ability to use QR codes which effectively makes it useless.

Here is the breakdown of different features available for verified vs. unverified subscription and service accounts:

Account type vs. Functionality	Unverified subscription account	Verified subscription account	Unverified service account	Verified service account
Message displayed in sessions list	✗	✗	✓	✓
Message displayed in subscription folder	✓	✓	✗	✗
Send 1 message per day	✓	✓	✗	✗
Send 4 messages per day	✗	✗	✓	✓
Basic function: receive/reply	✓	✓	✓	✓
Customized menu	✗	✓	✓	✓
Advanced features	✗	✗	✗	✓
WeChat payment	✗	✗	✗	✓

Marketing with WeChat can essentially be split into two stages:

1. Getting followers,

2. Keeping the followers engaged.

Strategies and methods for each stage are quite different: the first one taking place primarily off-platform while the second – within WeChat itself.

First stage: getting WeChat followers

The most straight forward way to get followers is by having them to scan WeChat account's QR code.

Here are the primary methods on how to accomplish that.

Publish QR code on your sites and social media

Every online channel that you company owns has should display QR code of your WeChat account as prominently as possible. Some sites go as far as setting it up in the header area or as a floating widget that always stays in view while scrolling. At the very minimum, the QR code should be at the footer that shows up on every page of the site.

Here is the screenshot from Starbucks Chinese website:

Add WeChat QR to all outgoing emails

Make sure to add QR code to all of your email communications, especially newsletters. It can be combined with announcing special offers that are available only to brand's WeChat followers. Such placement is another example of making QR code available to be scanned, and, at the same time, giving the readers a reason to scan it.

Also, keep in mind that emails are often viewed on mobile phones where QR code can be saved as a picture and loaded to WeChat application later on.

请通过微信公众号与我们联系

QR code on packaging

Including QR code on product packaging is another great opportunity for WeChat marketing. For example, scanning a code could connect a user to a customer service provided via WeChat official channel or offer a discount or a coupon for this or other product.

Run WeChat marketing campaigns in print

Traditional newspapers and magazines can be another great venue to place QR code at. They can also be combined with offers and discounts – an efficient way to entice people to scan it and become your brand's followers. Of course, printed media can be utilized in both large scale, such as posters and billboards, as well as be as small as a business card.

Another often overlooked idea is printing QR codes on sales receipts that are given to customers like in this example:

WeChat marketing at events

Events, such as trade shows, conferences and product launches provide ample opportunities to place WeChat QRs and encourage visitors to scan them. A simple roll up posters with an offer and a large QR code is the simplest and cost effective way to promote your WeChat official account to large crowds. Keep in mind, however, that if you are going to offer a free gift to everyone who scans your code, you'll get a lot of followers quickly but may lose large part of them as soon as they get a free gift.

Setting up some type of a lucky draw would be a more cost effective way to do that.

Get creative with QR codes

QR codes have just one drawback – they are ugly! Having a tiny logo in the center still doesn't improve their visual appeal. Fortunately, thanks to the new technology developed by Israeli company Visualead, it doesn't have to be that way anymore.

Visualead provides online QR generator to combine a QR code with any imagery, such as a logo or a picture. Here is an example of such picture based QR which is still perfectly scannable, just like its boring black and white equivalent:

Here are some more ways to get followers:

Share content for free gift

An example of effective WeChat marketing is encouraging customers to share a piece of content from your account in their WeChat moment. For example, a restaurant could offer to patrons a free desert or a discount off the bill if they present a proof of sharing a photo of a restaurant or a meal with their friends.

WeChat marketing with virtual loyalty card

Offering a virtual loyalty card in WeChat is another way to get more followers and can also become an effective WeChat marketing strategy. Owners of such loyalty cards can have their QR code scanned at the business location for discounts or points collection. Here is an example of such virtual card used by Wagas, a popular western restaurant in China:

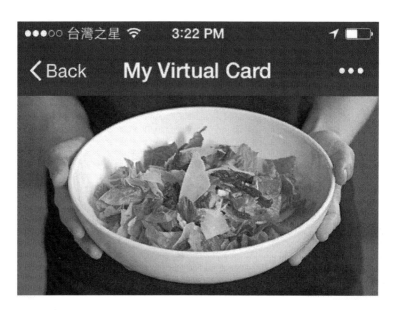

Scan your unique membership QR code
every time you make purchases at Wagas
and Baker & Spice. Earn one point per every
RMB spent on full priced items*.

WA003656

Free Wi-Fi to WeChat followers

WeChat official accounts now have a feature that allows displaying the closest Wi-Fi network directly in users' contacts. This feature works great with businesses that have a physical location, such as stores and restaurants. Prompting users to connect to a free Wi-Fi in exchange for signing up as a follower is another opportunity for effective WeChat marketing.

Create viral content and KOLs

Of course, creating viral content is easier said than done but getting followers sharing your WeChat posts or the account with their contacts is another way to get more followers. In fact this is precisely the way KOLs (key opinion leaders) operate. KOLs would share your content through their network of devoted followers to have them follow the account this way. KOLs is a lucrative industry in China with the popular ones making huge amounts of money off the deals with brands to promote their content.

This method has been most effective with fashion and luxury brands, although it is quickly spreading to other areas.

Don't delay communicating with followers!

There is a feature of WeChat official accounts that is known as "48 hours rule". It means that you only have 48 hours to engage with a follower directly after he/she subscribed to your channel or communicated to it via sending a message. It is important not to miss the opportunity to connect with a new follower within that time frame. Offering targeted content such as a coupon or a personalized invitation to an event would keep new followers engaged and minimize chances of losing them.

Every new follower is a potential sales lead and it is in your best interest to keep that lead hot. After all, unsubscribing from a WeChat channel is always just "a swipe" away.

Marketing within WeChat groups

One of the most often overlooked WeChat features for marketers is WeChat groups where members can participate in discussions. Inviting customers to join a group can be an effective way to keep them engaged with a brand. Each group is issued a unique QR code that users can scan in order to join, however, as soon as the group reaches its maximum allowed capacity (currently 100) scanning QR code would no longer work. An easy workaround to bypass this limit is to send an invitation to users to join a group – a group owner can invite unlimited number of participants to a group.

Second stage: engaging WeChat followers

Once your WeChat marketing is past the first stage of acquiring followers, the second stage is all about keeping them engaged and, ultimately, converting them to paying customers.

Here are the most common strategies to achieve these goals.

Optimizing content for WeChat

Although, reusing content from other social media channels or blogs for WeChat could be a time saver, the posts are often not optimized for this platform. For example, articles that are too long or those relying too much on the graphics may not render well on WeChat's smartphone screen. In other words, reusing content from other social media channels may not help in retaining WeChat followers.

One of the keys of WeChat marketing is figuring out the posts format that is just right in both size and layout. The graphics should be clear enough while displayed as a thumbnail in multiple picture posts while not looking pixelated when extended to the full screen. That would require some tweaking and testing to get everything right.

Also, if there are external links, they should lead to responsive pages that are optimized for mobile.

Videos are another medium that can significantly increase engagement with WeChat followers. Chinese mobile networks speed continues to improve making watching videos without Wi-Fi a much smoother experience than it used to be in the past.

Suitability for WeChat readers

When posting in WeChat, it is important to always keep in mind the mobile nature of the network. Since the posts will be consumed on mobile devices, they should be of the appropriate size and formatted for small mobile screens. What is normally suitable for web-based blogs is often too long for mobile, therefore, while recycling content from other platforms, you should consider trimming the content or splitting it into several posts.

People on mobile networks are often on the go and therefore prefer smaller and more digestible chunks of information. Reading text-heavy informative articles may be perfectly appropriate for a blog but not for a mobile network.

Retaining WeChat followers often requires posting messages that are more visual. It is often as easy as inserting images along with the text. Images can link to other content in the same WeChat account or external resources that would be opened inside WeChat browser (clicking on links inside WeChat doesn't take users out of the app as it is the case with most other apps).

Submission forms within WeChat should be tested with the smallest possible screen to make sure that they are easy to fill out and navigate for users on those type of mobile devices.

Targeting specific users or groups

Targeting enables improving content relevancy to a specific group of people and therefore, also helps with retaining WeChat followers.

Despite the fact that WeChat already knows a lot about its users, at the moment, the platform lacks most targeting options that are available with other social networks. However, it is still possible to achieve some targeting based on user location and gender. This can be done automatically within the platform while posting a message to followers.

More granular segmentation can be done manually by separating different users into groups that can be targeted with customized content. There are also 3rd party solutions that can achieve that based on different patterns of user behavior within your official WeChat accounts (e.g. their click and view history) as well custom parameters that can be defined by account admin.

While sending messages to followers in a specific location, you should keep in mind that WeChat only registers location based on the last user-initiated communication. For example, if a follower scanned QR code while in Beijing and never interacted with the account since that time – Beijing will become the default location, even though he or she could already be elsewhere. When the same user interacts with the app while in Shanghai, that will become the latest known location for the purposes of geo-targeting.

O2O campaigns

O2O, which stands for Online to Offline (or, sometimes Offline to Online) has been one of the hottest topics in marketing in the last couple of years. It has been identified as a trillion dollar opportunity by TechCrunch as well as called the industry's stupidest acronym by Tech in Asia. While some marketers still disagree on how the term should be used, O2O in China has been growing by leaps and bounds and is getting ahead of most other markets.

Basically, anything in the digital world that brings customers to the physical stores or makes them buy products and services that are traditionally sold offline can be classified as O2O.

WeChat has been one of the primary drivers of O2O in China with many brands designing campaigns that exploit this concept. For example, offering to WeChat followers a free gift that can only be collected in a physical store at specific location is just one example of O2O and how it can be used with mobile.

According to the recent report by McKinsey on O2O in China, it has been growing the fastest in 3 areas: travel, mobility and dining services:

Despite creating high expectations for discounts, O2O services strongly stimulate total spending.

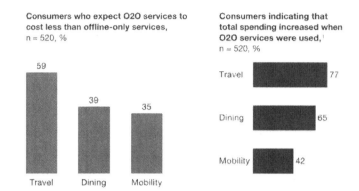

Consumers who expect O2O services to cost less than offline-only services, n = 520, %

Consumers indicating that total spending increased when O2O services were used,[1] n = 520, %

Travel 77
Dining 65
Mobility 42

Travel 59
Dining 39
Mobility 35

[1]Including those who answered "start doing," "total spend increases a lot (>50%)," and "total spend increases a bit (20–50%)."

McKinsey&Company | Source: McKinsey iConsumer China 2016 survey

Here are the main reasons behind O2O popularity with China's mobile users:

Sheer number of smartphones

Large number of smartphones in China is the primary reason for O2O services getting strong foothold. There are estimated 563 million smartphone users in 2016 representing more than a quarter of users worldwide.

Smartphone as the primary internet access point

Another factor in favor of O2O in China is the fact smartphones have long become the primary device of getting online for the majority of Chinese, beating desktops and laptops 2 years ago. Since large part of O2O's appeal is location, mobile is a natural fit.

Mobile payment systems

Proliferation of secure and convenient mobile payment systems such as Alipay or WeChat Pay has become the industry enabler. In this regard, China is well ahead of most other countries.

Everyone in China loves QR

QR codes can be used in many creative ways to facilitate O2O based connections and, incidentally, they have been extremely popular in China. While QR codes were declared dead in the West on more than one occasion, they have been embraced in China and popularized by apps like WeChat.

Quizzes and lucky draws

People like games and Chinese are no exception. Even more than games, people like winning prizes. Therefore, many successful WeChat campaigns have been incorporating all types of lucky draws, quizzes and virtual scratch cards. These methods can also be used in combination with various O2O campaigns mentioned earlier.

Marketing approach based on gamification of user experience has been proven exceptionally effective within WeChat environment giving rise to development of 3rd party WeChat extensions just for this purpose.

Coupons, discounts and free gifts

Offering discounts, coupons and free gifts is the most straight forward way to keep the followers interested and engaged. As with the previously described methods, these strategies can be incorporated into O2O campaigns by connecting digital offers to a physical point of sale.

In addition, if WeChat account runs its own store, discounts and coupons can be redeemed directly.

Exclusive WeChat sales

Ever since introduction of WeChat Pay, the built-in payment system, WeChat ecommerce has been growing at astonishing rate. It is now believed to be behind only two of the industry giants: Alibaba's Taobao/Tmall and JD.com. The majority of WeChat stores are focused on fast moving goods, fashion and luxury.

In fact, some of the top luxury brands that already had strong presence on WeChat, are now selling exclusively on this platform. Most recently, Coach even went as far as closing down their main Tmall store in favor of WeChat platform.

Why are some brands narrowing their ecommerce presence rather than expanding it? The explanation lies in brands' drive to focus on exclusivity rather than reach.

Companies in other industries, such as popular cellphone makers, often run flash sales of new hot models exclusively on WeChat creating the same type of effect.

Loyalty programs

One of the best ways to make sure your customers continue following your WeChat channel is setting up a loyalty or rewards program entirely based within the account. Such setup would allow members to use virtual cards at physical points of sale, accumulate rewards, check the balance and redeem the points.

Smartphones with WeChat app are already replacing physical wallets for millions of users. Digitizing traditional plastic loyalty cards by moving them to WeChat is seen as the part of the process of ditching wallets.

Common Misconceptions about WeChat Marketing

While WeChat can be a powerful marketing tool in China, it's important to realize what it can and cannot do. The best use of WeChat is to deploy it as one of the marketing elements, closely integrated with other channels, not in isolation.

Here are some common misconceptions about WeChat marketing:

No one else can use my brand

Many popular brands who are just getting around starting their WeChat marketing campaigns in China often find out that someone else is already using their brand name and logo. Once the account has been created by someone it can be quite hard to have WeChat to remove it. However, ignoring the problem is not a good idea either.

If, following the complaint, the owner of "squatter" account is refusing to comply by changing their WeChat account's name and logo, it is possible to file a complaint to Tencent accompanied with proper paperwork. In order to be successful, the legitimate brand owner has to prove their ownership of the trademark in China which is the whole new topic.

In-app mobile advertising within WeChat is effective

In fact, advertising within WeChat is notoriously ineffective while being also extremely expensive. Click through rate (CTR) of such ads is usually quite low for a number of reasons. The main problem is that once clicked, the user than will be taken out of the app elsewhere, usually to a built-in WeChat browser. Since most people don't casually browse WeChat but have some purpose while using it, they wouldn't typically abandon their activity in the middle to be redirected elsewhere.

The ads within user's Moments (WeChat's version of feed), are also rarely relevant and are not displayed consistently.

WeChat marketing allows accurate targeting

I wish that one was true. Unfortunately, it is quite difficult to segment WeChat marketing messages, which is also true for its advertising. On the most basic level, the followers can be segmented only by their location and gender. Even the location is based on whatever WeChat subscriber has set and not on the actual geolocation. Whenever a more granular approach is needed, each individual follower can be tagged and grouped. This would allow sending more targeted messages to a specific audience.

Such segmentation can be both manual – often an extremely time and labor consuming effort, or automated with some 3rd party backend platform customization. The biggest disadvantage of the platform, as compared to other popular social media channels, is its lack of tools to target followers based on their behavior, a crucial component in many effective digital marketing strategies.

Sina Weibo

Marketing on Weibo

Sina Weibo is one of the major Chinese social media platforms that used to be the largest and most active networks up until the rise of WeChat.

Despite losing large number of users to other networks, primarily to WeChat, Sina Weibo remains one of the most important online marketing platform. It is also undergoing gradual evolution which helps the network to stay relevant.

Although, the number of Weibo registered users has plateaued in the last 2 years, the number of daily and monthly users continues to increase. In September 2015, MAU (monthly active users) reached 227 million which represents 33% growth compared to the previous year. DAU (daily active users) for the same period was at impressive 100 million – 30% yearly increase.

In 2016, Weibo wasn't adding too many users and in fact, may have even shrunk after the company undertook efforts to clean it up by deleting thousands of "zombie" accounts.

In recent years, Weibo has managed to successfully reposition itself from primarily desktop based platform to a mobile one. Its mobile app is quite popular and the source of more than half of the network's traffic. In fact, people between 17 and 33 years old, who also represent the most active user base, are 83% mobile.

The platform has positioned itself as a discovery based network which makes marketing on Sina Weibo a natural choice. This is in contrast with the larger WeChat that is still primarily used as one-to-one communication tool. Much more private nature of WeChat doesn't allow the same type of discovery as Weibo does. This fact makes Weibo much more attractive to marketers and, as a result, the largest part of the service's revenue comes from its various advertising programs.

Network's ability to target users more accurately based on their interests and behaviors is what boost the effectiveness of marketing on Weibo.

Moreover, Weibo users tend to be quite educated. According to the latest data, over three quarters of users hold higher education degree. No such statistics is available for WeChat.

In terms of age distribution, almost 80% of Weibo users are between 17 and 33 years old. Only 13% are 34 and older.

A few years ago, Sina Weibo was only popular in 1st and 2nd tier cities. Lower tiers still preferred Tencent Weibo at the time. This has also changed – Sina Weibo has achieved roughly equal popularity and market share across all city tiers. This trend could also be attributed to the fact that Tencent's WeChat is gradually cannibalizing Tencent Weibo.

Weibo paid membership has also been on the rise. VIP user base has risen by 60% in Q3 2015 compared to the same period a year ago. According to Sina, revenues from VIP membership fees in 2015 exceeded USD 15M.

2015 has also seen a closer cooperation between Sina Weibo and Alibaba, its strategic partner which has also become one of the network's largest shareholders. It is expected that, at some point, Sina Weibo will become more integrated with Alibaba's e-commerce platforms like Taobao and Tmall.

Published content on Sina Weibo has also become more diverse. Previously, the main Weibo' topics used to be mostly news, media, business and celebrities. Now, the more diversified content covers movies, books, games, arts, lifestyle and other areas – another reason why marketing on Sina Weibo can be a more suitable choice for brands.

Here are a few tips on how to build your Weibo marketing strategy for maximum efficiency:

Setting up attractive Weibo page

Setup an attractive Weibo page. There are several Weibo templates that are free but it is always better to use your own unique theme that should match your corporate colors. You can browse Weibo pages of famous brands to get some ideas and inspiration for your own design.

Posting engaging content

Make sure to have your content relevant and frequently updated. You can also pre-write posts to be automatically published by an app like t.pp.cc. Refrain from dry promotional material, instead, write original and engaging posts. Keep in mind that the most shared content on Weibo are jokes, so injecting some humor would also be a good idea.

Posting videos

Post videos on a regular basis. People love watching and sharing clips but make sure that you don't post links from YouTube as they wouldn't open to a user from China. In later section, I'm going to review the local alternative to YouTube – Youku.

Monitoring posts' quality

Make sure your posts are proofread by a native Chinese speaker. Never ever use automatic translation for your English content! Such posts would look ridiculous – poorly written content is a major turn off for your audience.

Replying to comments

Engage with the audience by replying to comments and make sure to address negative ones as well. Always stay polite and professional in your comments but if some comments are truly abusive you can file a complaint to Weibo admin.

Engaging with selected followers directly

In some cases use private messaging feature to reply to some of your commentators and followers directly. This would build trust and boost your credibility.

Using

Just like Twitter, Weibo uses #hashtags to trace topics. If you use them effectively your posts may get better visibility too. Check other relevant posts to see which hashtags are popular at the moment.

Syncing your updates across all channels

Share your Weibo tweets on your website which can be done automatically with plugins and external services. This would bring more traffic and more followers.

Sina Weibo main functionality

The main Weibo features can be seen as a combination of Twitter and Facebook/Google+ functionality. Here are the most important ones:

Tweets

Tweets, or status updates, are limited to 140 characters limit. That number is clearly borrowed from Twitter which was, historically, related to SMS message limit and has become one of the most distinctive Twitter features and de-facto standard of micro-massaging. In Weibo's case, this limit has little relevance in Chinese language: due to the nature of the language, one can pack much more content in 140 Chinese characters than with 140 English letters.

Referencing topics

Similar to Twitter and unlike Facebook, topics can be referenced with #hashtags. The only difference in Weibo is that hashtags should surround word from both sides like this: #hashtags#.

Referencing people

Referencing other people or organizations with Weibo accounts is done with @, just like it is common with Facebook and Twitter. Reposts/retweets are done in the same way.

URL shortening

Most popular URL shortening services like bit.ly are blocked in China. All links are automatically shortened with Weibo's own service t.cn.

Media

Almost all types of rich media can be inserted with posts. That includes graphics, sounds and videos.

Commenting

Commenting on posts is similar to Facebook with comments appearing below the posts. When quoting, users can choose to include the original post in the comment

Here is an example of a home page of a corporate account:

Status update is at the top and this is where one can type in a message, insert emoticons and links as well as include pictures or videos.

Basic accounts statistics in top right corner show the number of followers, number of accounts you follow and number of published tweets.

Blue V indicates that the account has been verified with blue Vs reserved for organizations and yellow Vs for individuals. Verification is an important process that Weibo encourages accounts to go through. In case of companies, it is pretty much the norm and is required for almost any type of promotion activities on Weibo.

In the center, right below status update section, is the **newsfeed** section which is generated from either the followed accounts or sponsored ads.

On the right, there is a section featuring suggestions on the **accounts to follow**, they are automatically selected by Weibo based on your interests, topics you already follow as well as tweets history.

Here is an example of a corporate Weibo account of Alibaba Group:

Recently, Weibo has been cleaning up some design clutter and now the accounts look a bit more structured, although, some say, visually less interesting than in the past. The top part with the logo and cover image now resembles Google+

but the bottom is more in line with Facebook style, although the positions of the panels with newsfeed and ads are reversed.

Here is another example of a celebrity personal page of Alibaba's CEO Jack Ma:

In fact, the structures of both corporate and personal pages are very similar, however corporate accounts allow higher degree of design optimization.

Advertising with Weibo

Advertising and brand promotion on Weibo is quite different from Facebook and Twitter in the following ways:

- On Weibo there are no any targeted advertisements which show up anywhere outside of the newsfeed stream. This means that Weibo is much more similar to Twitter – all the messages, including the ads, show up in-stream. Essentially, advertising this way becomes more about content marketing. On the other hand, it is generally more difficult to capture the target audience accurately enough.

- Weibo's in-stream advertising product is called "Fensi Tong" which has two pricing models: first one is CPM (cost per thousand impressions) which is currently priced at 5 RMB per CPM. The second model is based on number of interactions with the ad: clicks, forwarding the ad, following the advertiser and saving the ad. This model uses bidding system, which similar to Google AdWords with the minimum bid currently set at 0.5 RMB per interaction.

- The advertising model that is unique to Weibo is based around KOLs (Key Opinion Leaders). Those are individuals who have millions of followers and their posts, in effect, become the advertisements that attract a lot of impressions and retweets. There are several levels of KOLs on Weibo marked with a capital "V" of different color representing user type after their names. For example, the orange "V" stands for an individual user while the blue "V" is reserved for group user such as a company, an organization or a media outlet. Reaching out to KOLs in your field and developing relationship with them is always, by far, the most efficient brand building strategy.

When it comes to pure advertising, Weibo offer these three basic options:

- Weibo Fans headlines (粉丝头条)

- Weibo Fans pass (粉丝通)

- Weibo Micro task (微任务)

Weibo Fans Headlines

This is the simplest way to promote a post by pushing it to the top of followers' feed. At present, Weibo charges 2.37

RMB per post to be displayed above others in the feed for 24 hours. There is 40% discount for any posts that mention anything related to Weibo itself.

Making a post more prominently displayed can be an effective way to attract clicks from brand followers by having them notice the content as soon as they log in. The obvious disadvantage is the fact that it only improves your content's visibility with your existing followers and does little to acquire new ones. On the other hand, the price for this type of promotion is fairly affordable.

Fans Pass

This type of promotion involves an ad campaign and can be initiated and managed with the advertising account. The advertising account opening process requires local ID and usually takes about 3 days to complete the approval process.

There are two pricing models: CPM (cost per thousand impressions) and CPE (cost per engagement) which are determined by automated bidding process, similar to the familiar Google AdWords.

CPM prices start at 5 RMB per CPM and can be increased by bidding up with 0.1 RMB increments.

"E" in CPE type of Weibo advertising stands for "engagement" that can be either click, a forward, a like or a follow. The initial price is set to minimum 0.5 RMB per CPE and can be increased at 0.01 RMB increment. The final price will ultimately be determined by quality of the content and competitive offers. If the price is set too low and the content is not engaging enough, the ad may not receive enough exposure, so setting the right bid and making adjustment to the content takes a bit of tweaking.

Weibo ad account provides some analytics tool to judge the effectiveness of an ad campaign but finding the right combination of all the parameters takes some skills and experience.

Micro task

The third type of promotion, which is also unique to Weibo, is called Micro Task and involves engaging KOLs, or Key Opinion Leaders.

KOLs are basically people with a lot of followers and are considered to be authority figures in their areas of expertise. Some KOLs have millions of followers which enables them to broadcast a targeted message to a very large audiences.

Depending on a specific industry, Weibo offers a range of KOLs to choose from. Typically, those with the largest following are more expensive to engage.

Working with KOLs requires opening an account and paying a deposit that is currently set to 2,000 RMB for companies. Once a suitable KOL is chosen, you can set a task (hence the name of this feature – "micro-task") that normally involves posting your content in KOLs feed that should appear at the time of your choosing and remain visible for a set period.

This is the example of KOLs which are suggested by Weibo for a specific topic:

Depending on a specific KOL and the type of promotion task he/she receives, the price is set by Weibo automatically.

Individuals (as opposed to companies) can also use micro-task to promote posts. There is no deposit for individual accounts and you pay as you go per each task. On the other hand, individuals can't pick KOLs which will be assigned by Weibo automatically.

Douban

Douban is one of the lesser known social medial platforms in China which has been around since 2005 and still enjoys widespread popularity. It has about 60 million registered and about 150 million unregistered users. In fact, one of the unique features of the network is the fact that users, who are not registered, can still enjoy 90% of the site's functionality.

Of course, compared to Weibo, WeChat, Renren or Qzone, those are fairly small numbers but what sets Douban apart is the unique culture created by the core of dedicated users. Unlike Weibo, it appeals to white collar, sophisticated Chinese urbanites. According to Doctor Yang Bo, the founder of Douban, most of the users live in major big cities of China. They are office workers, artists, freelancers and students who share common interests in arts, culture and lifestyle.

Douban is a truly unique Chinese social media phenomenon which can be loosely described as a sophisticated hybrid of Amazon's book reviews, IMDB.com, Blogger, MySpace, Pandora and Pinterest wrapped up into one platform.

The main core of the site is its communities grouped into:

- **Books section**, where people review and discuss books and can buy them directly from Chinese version of Amazon. It is one of the revenue sources for Douban;

- **Movies section**. This one is similar to imdb.com (which is periodically blocked in China) and is the main forum for movie reviews and latest gossip. Here users can book tickets and even book seats in cinemas nearby;

- **Music section** is, perhaps, the most popular one and it provides a platform for young musicians to post and promote their works. It is somewhat similar to what MySpace is all about these days.

The other part of the site features **Groups** which are, in turn, categorized by interests such as fashion, entertainment, photography, technology or lifestyle.

Next section is called City which features various events nearby, such as festivals, exhibitions, film screenings, theater performances etc. There is a section for people willing to get together for games, group shopping, dating or any other local activity.

Next one is **Douban.FM** which is a music streaming service. In its structure and functionality it is similar to Pandora. It streams music that matches listener's taste based on his/her history of favoring or skipping tracks.

In its latest attempt to generate more revenue, Douban has added a section simply called **Stuff** (东西) which is still in beta. It is all about discovering and shopping for cool things but it is quite unlike a bazaar style of Taobao. The closest Western equivalent would be Fancy.com which resembles Douban Stuff's type of merchandise and presentation. Items can be reviewed by users, favored, added to wish list or a shopping card and purchased. The Stuff section is somewhat a fresher and more sophisticated version of an online shopping site targeting buyers looking for individual style and less focused on searching for the cheapest bargains.

In the past, Douban has been criticized for slow user base growth as well as for failing to properly monetize its service by restricting its ads. It is true that advertising options are somewhat limited on the community pages with very little screen real estate dedicated to ads. Also, those spots tend to be quite expensive selling between 15 to 20 RMB per CPM, an order of magnitude higher than on comparable sites.

With the addition of the new Stuff section, Douban seems to have found a potentially lucrative formula to keep its distinct and sophisticated character and yet take advantage of the desire of the urban elite, its main user base, to express their individuality through buying unique things.

Overall, in terms of marketing value, Douban seems to be one of the most underrated Chinese social media sites with great potential. Besides of obvious option of promoting products through its new Stuff section, Douban could be an excellent venue for a more sophisticated marketing campaign targeting upscale urban consumers through its communities and groups platform.

Several high brands have also established what is called a brand stations on Douban. One example is of Adidas that features its collections but also actively promoting the brand through completions and events.

For example, visitors and followers get engaged in viewing and commenting on user generated content that feature Adidas brands that is often unique and visually appealing. Below are just a few examples from Adidas brand station on Douban:

User generated content featuring Adidas brand:

Originals 艺术合作 (注释)

Video stories on artists creating "Adidas inspired" art:

Originals 影像空间 (条约)

艺术家之椅- Came Chau创作故事
艺术家之椅- 官纯创作故事
艺术家之椅- 唐彦创作故事

Corporate content featuring Adidas latest collection:

Contest by Adidas prompting users to submit their stockings and socks footwear matching design:

In conclusion, Douban, being a one of a kind social media site in China, is often overlooked by marketers as an alternative venue to appeal to increasingly sophisticated big city based users. It has recently developed more marketer-friendly platforms and tools that can be effectively used to target this fast growing sector of Chinese online community.

Professional networks

Chinese professional networking sites have been the fast growing sector in the last few years. With the largest labor market in the world, China still offers a very attractive opportunity for such platforms. However, this space has been undergoing some significant changes since 2015.

First and most recently, Viadeo, the LinkedIn competitor, has decided to pull the plug on their Chinese site called Tianji.com. In its recently released announcement, Viadeo explained that the move was necessary in order to consolidate their resources on more profitable sectors, such as their home French speaking market, both in France and in other francophone countries.

Although, Tianji.com has reached 25 million users, the development resources required to maintain and expand the platform just weren't available, according to the company.

Then there were significant challenges related to platform's adaptability to mobile which would require even more investment.

Finally, following recent economic slowdown in China, Viadeo has failed to secure the local partner or a strategic investor who would help to develop the network further.

As a result, Tianji.com's service has been stopped leaving millions of registered users out in the cold.

Another one of the major Chinese professional networking sites, Ushi.cn, has also called it quits in early 2016. Ushi has been designed to resemble LinkedIn in both layout and functionality, although it failed to attract enough users to be able to compete with larger networks. The service has been shut down without any announcement. Estimated 2 million users, many of them foreigners who were looking to build networks in China, have seen their efforts in setting up profiles and connecting with others wasted as well.

On the other hand, US based LinkedIn has been slowly gaining momentum in China, perhaps also learning from the mistakes of the competitors who tried to build Chinese professional networking sites on top of their existing platforms.

First, LinkedIn has managed to secure significant investments from with Sequoia China and CBC (China Broadband Capital). Second, it was successful in getting support from both Tencent, the company behind WeChat, and Sina Weibo – two largest social networks in China. For example, WeChat and LinkedIn profiles can now be linked which can potentially boost LinkedIn exposure to mobile users.

Finally, unlike Google and Facebook, LinkedIn has agreed to play by local rules. User generated content will have to comply with censorship regulations in the same way it works with other Chinese social networks through combination of automated filters and human censors.

Also, some of the popular LinkedIn tools will not be available to Chinese users. Those will include automated cross postings via Twitter, creating and joining groups, posting long essays and participating in online public discussions. What would LinkedIn look like without those features remains to be seen.

Other Chinese professional networking sites still seem to be around. Two of the most popular ones, Dajie and Renhe are still live and doing well. Dajie, the largest of them, claims to have over 32 million registered users vs. Renhe's 7 million. Both sites have also expanded their mobile presence with apps for Android and iOS.

Dajie.com, the largest network is mostly popular with fresh graduates and its users tend to be younger with large percentage of job seekers. Therefore, it doesn't seem to be the right venue for companies looking to reach top level executives and decision makers. However, the platform may still provide lucrative opportunities for educational sector. If your objective is promoting your educational programs, from language courses to MBA programs, Dajie should certainly be looked at as one of such marketing platforms.

On the other end of the spectrum, Renhe.cn tends to cater to white color professionals and executives focusing primarily on financial sector. This network can be a suitable platform for marketing to professionals but its focus on financial sector could somewhat limit the range of brands, products and services that can be marketed efficiently. On the positive side, VIP membership (of up to 400 RMB per month for the highest level) offers number of features that can be useful in reaching executives and getting your message directly to targeted members. Company research capabilities are also quite advanced compared to similar platforms.

Unfortunately, Renhe seems to be a bit all over the place and hasn't yet found its specific niche. In any case, I'd recommend keeping an eye on it to see how it develops down the road and what marketing value it may be able to deliver.

Facebook

One of the unique features of Chinese digital marketing landscape compared to the rest of the world is seeming irrelevance of Facebook, one of the world's largest digital advertisers. As a result, Facebook marketing in China isn't a channel that marketers would typically consider adding to the mix. The platform has been blocked by Chinese government since 2009 and the only way to access it from the Mainland is by using VPN service.

Seven years of Facebook's absence in China gave more than enough time for local competitors to emerge and, ultimately, dominate the market. While some of the earlier Facebook Chinese clones fell into relative obscurity, WeChat and Weibo took the lead and have reached the position of almost unrivaled dominance.

As can be seen in this famous image of Facebook activity worldwide, China is the only major country that is completely from the map:

Does that mean that Facebook marketing is forever doomed in China? Not necessarily.

First of all, there is still a significant Facebook audience who uses VPN to access the platform regularly. The exact number is unknown because Facebook doesn't release statistics of users by country outside of US. Even if they did, VPN itself, by definition, makes it impossible to find out the actual traffic origin. It is however, safe to say that the vast majority of Chinese expat population still uses Facebook. The same is also true for a large proportion of sophisticated English speaking Chinese urbanities.

This means that if a company is looking to target this type of audience, Facebook marketing in China can still be an effective tool. Examples of common products and services advertised on Facebook in China include expat services (health insurance, visa services etc.), VPN services, local events and venues targeting foreigners and upscale Chinese and so on.

Secondly, Facebook never abandoned hopes of reentering the market with Mark Zuckerberg embarking on a charm offensive with the goal to make that happen. He has visited China multiple times and had personally met with the Minister of Propaganda, China's internet czar as well as Premier Xi Jingping himself. Mark Zuckerberg has even mastered a decent of level of Chinese surprising a lot of people by delivering speech in Mandarin in front of Chinese student audience followed by questions & answers session.

In this well publicized and mercilessly mocked photo, Zuckerberg was photographed running in Beijing despite Beijing's Air Quality Index climbing past 300 on that day:

Most analysts believe that Facebook return is just a matter of time, although it is unlikely to threaten the current local market leaders.

In fact, if Facebook ever relaunches in China, it will be a much more sanitized version of the network, forced to play by local rules that regulate everything from the content to who can use it for advertising. Chinese Facebook will most likely be quite different compared to the type of platform we are familiar with today.

If that eventually happens, advertisers will have to go through similar approval process as it is the case for local platforms like WeChat, Weibo or Baidu with locally registered businesses being favored compared to foreign ones. On top of Facebook's own guidelines, advertisers will have to comply with much stricter Chinese regulations that, over time, tend to get tighter rather than relaxed.

It is also very likely that Facebook, rather than going to China alone, will have to partner with a local company, perhaps even with one of its current competitors. This is often the case of large western companies entering Chinese market and is even more common for businesses in the areas social media or messaging like LinkedIn or Line.

Two more factors make Facebook return to China ever more likely: first, bringing back a censored and government-friendly version of Facebook will constitute a big victory for Chinese internet authorities, second, Mark Zuckerberg's indication of his willingness to compromise.

In any case, once Facebook is allowed back in China, it will most certainly become another effective marketing channel. Moreover, the competition for advertisers' dollars (or rather yuan) is also bound to intensify, hopefully resulting in more options and features from the existing channels like Weibo, Baidu and WeChat.

Leveraging social media KOLs

Engaging KOLs, which stands for Key Opinion Leaders, for product promotion in China is, almost always, one of the critical components in marketing strategy by big brands. The fact is that Chinese tend to trust information delivered via social media and, especially, by trustworthy people, much more than the one promoted via traditional channels. KOLs are, essentially, individuals or sometimes companies, who are active in social media and enjoy high degree of public trust and credibility. They could be very effective not only in delivering marketing messages to their audience but also making them feel more genuine.

In addition, numerous studies show that word of mouth is, many times, more effective than advertising. Hence, leveraging KOLs for brand marketing is becoming a way to harness that power.

Almost every big brand marketing in China involves, to some degree, using KOLs in their marketing campaigns. Most often those are celebrities, but, depending on the type of product being promoted, could also be influential bloggers and intellectuals.

In this section, I'm going to list the main ways big brands choose the right KOL for their marketing campaigns. Since some of the methods require hiring agencies and extensive research, not to mention considerable costs, they may not be suitable for smaller brands. In the following section, I'll make another list of down-to-earth methods that can be used by smaller companies, those without multimillion marketing budgets, to engage KOLs.

Methods of selecting KOLs by big brands

Determining most suitable KOL type

First off, companies should decide which type of KOLs best fits the product being marketed. Celebrities can be an obvious choice for high fashion and cosmetics but may not be suitable for other types of brands. Often, the best way to go is to engage a subject matter expert who specializes in a specific area and has recognized authority in the field. Such experts may not be a household name but can often be many times more effective than a celebrity.

Focus on authentic experience

Authenticity is quickly becoming the new buzz word in marketing and it basically means that in order to be effective, a marketing message has to carry high degree of credibility. Increasingly sophisticated consumers tend to distrust standard product endorsements putting more value into trustworthy opinion. One way to achieve that is to encourage KOLs to actually use the product and honestly express their experience.

Quality of fan base

One of the key definitions of social media KOLs, such as those on Weibo or WeChat, is the size of their fan base, or number of people following them. Numbers, however, do not tell the whole story. With the proliferation of fake accounts in social media as well as notorious services that claim to boost one's number of followers, marketers are forced to look more deeply into the quality of one's followers. There are some companies who develop complex mathematical models to measure KOL's influence. Also, Weibo itself has a scoring system that takes into accounts various parameters.

Virality and engagement

The key component in KOL's efficiency is their ability to generate "viral effect" with their messages, as well as keeping followers engaged. Clearly, tweeting a particular message to a large audience without it going further beyond the immediate followers would indicate that the message, or its delivery, wasn't effective. In such cases, engaging a KOL would unlikely to bring the expected value. As with the quality of fan base, there are tools and methods to judge the effectiveness of specific KOLs.

Covering events

One of the best ways to engage KOLs is to have them cover high profile events, such as product launches. Companies would often invite them to such events providing front row seats and other incentives. In addition, KOLs would have valuable opportunities to network and meet celebrities. They would be expected to write an account of their experience with some engaging content such as pictures and videos.

Engaging KOLs outside of social media

Big brands tend to build long lasting relationships with the most effective KOLs which go beyond social media presence. If there is a good fit between KOL's personality and the brand, such relationship can become brand's key marketing asset in the long run. They can also be employed with whatever future online or offline platforms that will be popular in the future.

When it comes to KOLs, companies with multimillion marketing budgets have wide variety of options, especially those involving securing endorsements of celebrities. Most of those methods would be out of reach for small businesses trying to expand their marketing in China through social media.

However, there are still relatively inexpensive ways to take advantage of KOLs on Weibo through a system called Weibo micro task (微任务). Next, I'm going to describe ways to choose a suitable KOL to engage and avoid common mistakes.

Weibo KOL score

Weibo provides some basic metrics on each KOL, which is registered in their database, such as number of followers and 6 star based score. How exactly the stars are assigned is not disclosed but it is assumed to be based on the power of influence rather than the number of followers. There are some KOLs with large fan base but low score and vice versa. The price is ultimately determined by the number of stars assigned to a particular KOL.

Quality of fan base

When KOLs are used for small business marketing, quality almost always takes precedence over quantity. Unfortunately, there are still many fake accounts, created specifically to boost someone's following. Obviously, working with KOLs with a lot of such zombie fans would be a complete waste of your marketing budget. Doing your due diligence on the fan base is not easy but you should look out for a few red flags, such as low star score (i.e. inexpensive to engage) but too many followers or those that are new but managed to accumulate large fan base too quickly.

Relevance

Relevance to a product or service you are promoting is the most important parameter to consider when choosing KOL based on Weibo suggestions. It is almost always a good idea to stay away from KOLs whose blogs are either too general or cover very wide range of topics. Instead you should go with the ones that focus on the niche audience that you are targeting.

Geographical reach

In some cases, you may choose to target specific geography rather than running a nationwide campaign. In such cases, you should make sure that KOL, whom you are considering, covers that region or, better yet, focuses on it. Also, you could simply count the number of followers who come from the area that you are targeting.

KOL's style and tone

In order to judge whether a particular KOL is a good fit for your brand, it is best to simply read their posts. The style should match the marketing tone that you are trying to convey, be it humorous and lighthearted or serious and corporate. Also, it is worth reading further into the past to determine whether KOL's style has been consistent.

Engagement level

Although, Weibo's own scoring system is supposed to reflect this important parameter, it is something that is recommended to check as well. How often the posts are being re-tweeted? Do they generate comments? Does KOL respond to the comments in person? Clearly, it is not easy to go through thousands of posts to determine the engagement level, so I recommend using tools such as Hootsuite which now includes apps for digging into Weibo.

Involvement with other media

Influential KOLs are often present on multiple platforms, such as WeChat or have their own blog site. When determining authenticity and authority of a particular KOL, it is a good idea to check those other channels as well. Are they consistent? Do they cover same or related topics?

Develop closer relationship

As a next step, you can get in touch with KOL and establish relationship outside of Weibo. Encouraging them to personally try your product and write about their experience could go a long way in the long run.

Events

Once you have managed to establish offline relationship with the KOL, invite him/her to your events such as product launches or participation in trade shows. Covering it in their blog could become an excellent piece of PR for your company.

In conclusion, there are ways to maximize your KOL marketing campaign efficiency and navigate around common pitfalls. However, at the end of the day, it is still, to some degree, a trial-and-error process. My advice it to start small first and try few KOLs that look most promising, then measure the return. This way you will be able to figure out fairly quickly, and with the least cost, which one delivers the best value.

Other marketing channels: Videos, email marketing, banners ads

Videos

Watching and sharing videos through social media is one of the most frequent and beloved activities of a typical China's internet user. Due to YouTube's inaccessibility from the Mainland, Youku has been the main video hosting service in China for some time. Since Youku's merger with Tudou, the second largest video host, back in 2012, Youku-Tudou is estimated to hold about 60% of the total online video market share in China.

Statistics show that there were about 500 million online video users in China and this number has been steadily growing at the annual rate of between 12 to 15% since 2007.

Given such enormous reach and, traditionally, high degree of video consumers' engagement, advertising on this platform could be highly effective. In fact, according to Youku's financial reports, nearly 90% of its revenue comes from selling ads.

On the other hands, advertising on Youku is significantly different from YouTube in several key aspects.

More about brand advertising, less about direct marketing

Although some targeted advertising is available with Youku, the options are quite limited. As opposed to YouTube, the platform seems to be unable to target specific users based on their preferences or browsing history. Instead, Youku is still focused on blanket advertising by pursuing the largest possible audience, similar to traditional media such as TV or newspapers.

There is an inherent disadvantage of such approach: displaying Porsche ad to a student or a soccer mom would be a complete waste of Porsche's advertising dollars (not that we'd feel too sorry for them anyway…). It's reasonable to assume that Youku is working on smarter ways to display ads but, unfortunately to marketers, it isn't there just yet.

Limited value of the analytics

Just as with YouTube, Youku makes basic analytics available to its customers. The data includes viewers' demographics, geolocation, browsing technology, language, operating systems etc. As mentioned above, since the targeting options are not yet well developed, the practical value of such statistics has its limitations. It seems that Youku does know how to display ads relevant to what a viewer is presently watching but can't show them based on recent browsing history – something that YouTube or Google's AdSense does quite well.

Great multitude of ad options

The ads can be displayed in various shapes and forms: from videos to banners which can be both static or animated, as well as text links and buttons. Those are often referred to as "hard advertising". Other forms include product placements in in-house produced content, or branded viral videos all of which are collectively known as "soft advertising".

The price depends on the type of the ad, where and how it is displayed, and what scheme is chosen by a client. The most expensive ads are the ones that are displayed near the top of the page and those that are larger in size as opposed to smaller ones or those that are visible only after scrolling.

For big spenders only

Advertising prices didn't see significant changes since 2012 and they vary wildly depending on the type of ads.

There are two basic schemes:

- Banners in various locations on the site. Those can be quite expensive starting RMB 50K up to 300K per day depending on ads location and size. Here are the examples of such advertisement:

- Ads displayed with the video being watched which could be pre-roll, mid-roll and post-roll as well as pause ads. Those are CPM based and the prices typically range between 35 RMB/CPM to 330 RMB/CPM depending on type, length, geographic area and device.

Youku pre-roll ads: those are the ads that are displayed before the start of a video and they can't be skipped:

Mid and post-roll ads are displayed during the video at certain times or at the end of it, similar to TV commercials. Since they can be skipped by a viewer they will be priced at much lower rate than pre-roll ones.

Here is an example of a post-roll ad that is displayed at the end of a clip and will stay on until closed:

Youku pause ads are displayed whenever a video is paused. Such ad would stay on until playback is resumed. Those types of ads are usually static but can be quite effective – if the video is paused several times, a viewer will be seeing it every time which increases the impression rate per the same user.

Here is how a pause ad looks like:

Moreover, there is a nice feature of Youku that keeps a small floating frame of the video in constant view every time the page is scrolled down. This means that whenever a clip is paused, a pause ad will stay in view no matter where a user is on the page. Here is how that would look like:

Who are the typical advertisers?

According to Youku, the vast majority of the advertisers are producers of the fast-moving consumer goods (~50%); IT services and telecoms (~20%); internet services (~10%) with the rest of the 20% spread between automotive companies, financial services and some others. Youku works with fairly large number of globally-recognized companies such as P&G, Coca-Cola, General Motors, Apple as well as local heavyweights like China Mobile, e-commerce company Jingdong.com, food company Yum! etc.

In conclusion, Youku does offer a lucrative opportunity to reach extremely large audience but it doesn't come cheap. Also, the lack of focus on direct marketing makes Youku platform less suitable for companies seeking to target a specific audience. On the other hand, advertisers that could benefit less from accurate targeting, fast food chains for example, can see their advertising dollars well spent by using Youku platform.

Email marketing

Basics of email marketing for Chinese market

Well designed and properly executed email marketing campaign is often more cost effective than any other form of online advertising. This is why email marketing in China should always be considered as an important channel to reach your target audience.

Actually, emails have never enjoyed the same status in China as in the West because the country joined the internet revolution much later. Proliferation of messaging apps like QQ in the past and WeChat most recently, also offered much faster ways to communicate than emails. This, however doesn't mean that emails are irrelevant, quite the opposite. Studies show that most adults check their email inbox, on average, 40 times a day and often do it first thing in the morning. Also, with the right tools, emails are easy to track and analyze, enabling gathering data to make the subsequent campaigns even more effective.

Another consequence of the late adoption of emails in China is the fact that the vast majority of personal emails are hosted on just few domains of which about half are at QQ.com.

The biggest problem with email marketing in China (and with email marketing in general) is, of course, spam. Most countries around the world have introduced laws and regulations designed to limit amount of spam by specifying requirements to emails and imposing various degrees of penalties for violators. For example, federal anti-spam legislation CAN-SPAM Act of 2003 requires proper opt-out link to be included in a promotional mail, valid "from" email and a clear "subject" line.

Email marketing in China must also comply with complex China's anti-spam regulations. Chinese law stipulates substantial penalties for unsolicited emails and non-compliance may result in your IP address or domain getting blocked, making it inaccessible from the Mainland indefinitely.

Chinese anti-spam legislation of 2006 is called "Regulations on Internet Email Services" and is, by far, more complex and much stricter than its US equivalent. This law applies to emails sent to all Chinese residents and, at least in theory, also covers users who happened to receive emails while in Chinese territory.

According to the law, the penalty goes from 10,000 RMB and up to 30,000 RMB per email in case the violation involves "unlawful proceeds". The law doesn't specify what such "unlawful proceeds" might mean.

So, considering such tight restrictions and severe penalties, why would anyone even entertain the idea of mass email marketing campaign in China? Well, here is the upside: so far, there have been no known or, at least, reasonably high profile cases of the actual application of the law or prosecuting any offenders. In fact, the law does little to help with the major spam problem that exists today in Chinese internet space.

Obviously, one has to be aware of the legal aspect of email marketing in China and continue following common practices such as including unsubscribe link, acquiring and growing email mailing lists by legitimate means and, of course, staying away from sensitive topics. Violating such rules can have your domain blacklisted risking completely blocking your company's access to users in China. One should keep in mind that the famous China's Great Firewall is notoriously effective and you don't want to find yourself on the other side of it one day.

Here is the brief summary of the requirements to promotional emails according to the law:

Verifiable Permission

Chinese law requires recipient's explicit permission to be given in order to include an email in mass mailing list. Unsubscribe or opt-out option is not enough. The permission has to be verifiable and stored indefinitely in case of an audit.

Word "Ad" in subject line

Either English "Ad" for English language emails or the equivalent Chinese word for "advertisement" is required in the subject line.

Content requirements

Chinese promotional email definition is much broader than the one of CAN-SPAM Act and includes all kinds of messages containing any type of advertisement.

Downloadable content requirements

If a message contains any links to external content, such as a piece of software or an app, the law requires a written guarantee that they do not contain any spyware or anything that can facilitate hacking. It is not clear whether this applies to downloadable graphics such as images or thumbnail icons;

Content restrictions

Article 57 of the Regulations on Telecommunications stipulates the content of the allowable email which is purposefully left quite vague. There are thousands of words and topics that are currently banned and the list is very dynamic. Politically sensitive topics are the obvious examples as well as everything that is deemed obscene or pornographic. It's a good idea to refer to the list of blacklisted keywords in Wikipedia before starting your China email marketing campaign.

Although all of that sounds quite complicated, the good news is that if you pick a reputable EDM (email direct marketing) provider with experience in Chinese market, you don't have to worry about any of that. Such provider will also be able to ensure high rates of deliverability to most commonly used mailboxes in China: QQ.com, 163.com, 126.com, Sohu.com and Sina.com.

Unfortunately, most well-known EDM providers in Western market such as iContact, Mailchimp or ConstantContact, often experience problems delivering emails in China. This is why it is important to look for a provider which focuses on Chinese market and, ideally, can run campaigns from the servers that are located within the country.

Email templates and designs that work

When it comes to designing an email for Chinese email marketing campaign, there are few rules to keep in mind. Let's have a closer look at the main design elements of an email template.

Design elements

Images

The best eye catching email designs often include an image at the top. This would be the first and most visible part of the email, therefore it should always have a purpose. In some cases, a logo would do as long as it reinforces an already familiar brand.

Multiple marketing studies have long concluded that images with people (preferably attractive ones) are most effective. You should always think of what kind of mood the image conveys and whether it serves the intended purpose before choosing the right one.

Another technical aspect to keep in mind is setting a descriptive ALT tag to the image inside the HTML template in case the picture doesn't load for some reason.

Since the large proportion of recipients in China would use smartphones to check their emails, it is important to make sure that the details of the header picture are clearly visible once it has been shrunk to fit small screen. At the same time, it shouldn't take more than half of the mobile device's screen.

Overall picture size is another important consideration. Ideally, in order to load fast enough with relatively slow Chinese mobile networks, the images should not exceed 50KB without loss of quality.

Headline

Headline can be set either above or below the header image and should be short and concise enough with as few words as possible. Fortunately, since Chinese language allows to pack more meaning in smaller space, it is often easier accomplish than in English.

Headline copy doesn't have to be totally descriptive but as long as it is interesting or intriguing enough, it would serve as a "hook" to a reader encouraging them to take a closer look at the content.

Headline is extremely, if not the most, important element of a promotional email. This is why it is always a good idea to run a few headline versions by native Chinese speakers to gather some feedback before settling on the best one.

Call to Action

Call to Action or CTA as it is often abbreviated is, perhaps, the next most important element after the headline. Since it has to stand out, CTAs are often designed as buttons.

Research shows that red and orange buttons attract most clicks, although they should still match the overall design as to not look too much out of place.

Last thing you want is for an email recipient to be confused about what to do with it, this is why CTA is so critical. Best email designs often use clever imagery that would direct attention to CTA at unconscious level. For example, a person in an image could be facing or pointing in the direction of a CTA button. Amazingly enough, such subtle tricks work quite well.

Another tip is to include two CTAs in the email: one at the top and one at the bottom. The top one should work for people who get interested right away, so they wouldn't have to scroll all the way down to the bottom. However, the bottom placed CTA would be a more natural choice for those recipients who became engaged enough to read the entire content of the email.

Here is an example of an email template that contains many of the right elements discussed above – header image, catchy headline and clear CTA button (courtesy of EssayShark.cn):

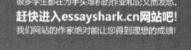

Main copy

We live under permanent information overload which causes us to constantly filter out information, both consciously and subconsciously. Nowadays, very few people possess enough patience to read long ads unless the content happens to be really important to them. In fact, very few people actually read emails rather than just scan them.

This is why the shorter the main copy – the better the results would be. Packing just enough content into ad copies that are as short as possible is an art in and of itself and it is something that is the absolute must for email marketing.

Ideally, the image, the headline, the copy and the CTA should appear "above the fold", in other words, displayed without having to scroll down the email. This can be quite challenging, especially in one column design for a smartphone. If it is not possible, consider showing at least the first and the most important paragraph at the top.

Mobile friendly design

As mentioned above, Chinese recipients would most likely read their emails on a smartphone. This is why it is important to make sure that the email renders properly with a smaller screen. It is most commonly achieved by responsive design which, nowadays, has become a de facto standard in web design.

In such designs, multi column emails are typically stretched into just one column. This is why you should make sure that the most important content, such as headline and CTA, appear at the top instead of being tucked down at the bottom.

Fortunately, larger screen smartphones are becoming more popular, easing some of the tight space constraints.

Note how the same email template renders on mobile with most of the important content showing above the fold:

Courtesy of EssayShark.cn.

Colors

Color perception varies from culture to culture and Chinese have their own preferences that may not always align with those of Westerners.

The colors that invoke similar reactions among Chinese and Westerners are:

1. Blue – is associated with high quality and trustworthiness;

2. Purple – reflects sophistication and high value;

3. Green – identifies with being pure and reliable.

Also, green in Chinese culture is not associated with "inexperience" as it is the case in Western subconscious perception.

This makes the above colors the safest choices for email marketing in China although they may not be impactful enough.

If you want to pack more punch, consider going with red and yellow – they are often considered more effective colors in China. Those colors have traditionally been associated with royalty and authority. Red in particular is the color of happiness, love and luck in China while for

Westerners it is subconsciously associated with danger, fear and anger.

Black is also perceived as a positive color in China while white has been the traditional color of death and mourning.

Content

The content of a promotional email is just as critical as its graphics and structure. Therefore, it is important to make sure that email's content complies with the rules and regulations that may be different in China compared to other jurisdictions.

General rules about content

Headline is, by far, the most important part of an email. There is much better chance for a recipient to continue reading the email if the headline appears interesting or intriguing enough rather than generic and bland. Everything that follows afterwards should be presented in the order of decreasing level of importance.

When it comes to content of promotional emails, less is always more. Reducing the volume of text without sacrificing the impact is not something that is easily achievable. However, the attempt to refine the content, simplify the language and keep the size to the minimum is well worth the effort.

The rules mentioned above are fairly universal and should be followed regardless of whether the campaign is for Chinese or international audience. However, choosing the proper tone of the main text copy does require taking into account cultural specifics.

In the West, it is considered to be popular to use informal, light and often humorous language in many marketing emails. This does not often translate well for Chinese readers. Adopting a tone that is too informal may actually convey a message of low level of commitment or poor quality. Using a reasonably formal or neutral language is typically the best choice for most brands.

Straight translation of English copy into Chinese rarely works well. This is why it is imperative to use professional native copywriters. They will make sure that the language is appropriate, respectful and avoids cultural references that are not widely understood in China.

Subject line

Subject line is what email recipient sees the first. The general rule here is for the subject line not to appear "spammy". Advertisers are constantly trying to come up with new ideas to "hook" the readers – from using intriguing questions to making outrageous claims in the subject lines.

Choosing the best performing subject line very much depends on the profile of both the business and the recipients. For example, a simple indication of what the message is about will do just fine for an existing mailing list of dedicated audience who are already familiar with the brand. However, for new recipients of an unfamiliar message, making subject line appearing less generic typically works better.

There are different opinions of the effectiveness of using special characters and icons in the subject line – some find it catchy and interesting while others can be put off by them. On average, using icons in subject line increases open rate but, on the other hand, some email filters may classify such emails as spam.

Most EDM providers have an option to run A/B split tests on different versions of the subject line. This is an effective way to figure out whether using special characters is a good idea for a given audience.

Word "AD" in subject line

Chinese antispam regulation requires all promotional email to include word "AD" or equivalent in the subject line. Failure to do so may get you fined and/or cause your domain to get banned and become permanently inaccessible in China.

Here is an example of how it is supposed to appear:

Courtesy of Apple Inc.

Links to downloadable content

It is best to avoid links to downloadable content such as apps or software. If the email must have such links, advertisers should also include a disclaimer stating that the downloadable content does not have spyware, malware or any other unsafe content.

It is a good idea to have such written document ready to be presented upon request from China's internet authorities.

What can and can't be legally promoted in China

Before starting an email campaign in China to promote a product or a service, it is critical to verify its local legal status. Currently, wide range of topics that are perfectly legal to advertise in other countries are either outright banned or fall into legal grey area in China. Of course, an experienced China focused EDM provider would be able to advise you on that, although it makes sense to check for any possible issues before investing in your Chinese email marketing.

For example, promotion of gambling, including online type, is strictly prohibited in China (with the exception of special administrative region of Macau). Marketing of alcohol and tobacco products are also prohibited as well as any adult content.

One of the most recently banned items include so called cryptocurrency. Although, most bitcoins are presently mined in China, as of August 2016, advertising anything related to bitcoin, including hardware and software for mining, became illegal.

Finally, when promoting events, advertisers must be especially careful to make it very clear that those have nothing to do with politics or religion.

Blacklisted keywords

Including any of the blacklisted keywords in email marketing campaign can cause serious problems for advertisers. This is why it is imperative to check the text against the list of currently blacklisted keywords which can be found in Wikipedia.

Politics is the most sensitive topic and, as mentioned before, should absolutely be avoided in any case. However, some "innocent" words could occasionally get blacklisted as well, especially if they inadvertently become euphemisms carrying a second meaning.

This is why the list of blacklisted keyword is fairly dynamic and grows over time, so what was OK yesterday, could get banned tomorrow.

Links to landing pages and social media

A promotional email can have a number of links. Most commonly, the primary link is the one of the CTA (call to action) that redirects readers to the landing page (LP). Considering the fact that most users in China use smartphones to read emails, it is very likely that they are also going to view LP inside their phone's mobile browsers.

This is the reason to make sure that LP renders properly on a small mobile screen without the need for a visitor to zoom it out in order to read it. Responsive design for LPs is equally important as for the email template itself. Unfortunately this part is frequently overlooked by advertisers.

If the LP design is not suitable for a mobile browser due to poor rendering or slow loading time, click through rate (CTR) of the email campaign will be effectively wasted further down the sales funnel.

Social media links can provide an additional source of followers and should certainly be included at the email footer unless those links are the principal CTA. Keep in mind, however, the different nature of social media landscape in China: there is little point to include Facebook, Twitter or YouTube links as they won't work in China anyway. Instead, consider including link to Weibo page and WeChat QR code.

When read on a desktop, a WeChat QR code can simply be scanned with a smartphone to follow a particular account. Unfortunately, it is not as straightforward for mobile users. In those cases, the reader has to be able to save QR code as a picture and then load it to WeChat in order to follow that particular account. This is quite cumbersome process for most users and unless they are really invested into finding your WeChat account, most would probably skip that step.

Hopefully, in the future, WeChat could offer an easier way to follow accounts directly from emails but, as of the time of this writing, we are not there yet.

Banner advertising

Banner ads in China are still a fairly effective channel to advertise and, on average, Chinese are more receptive to this type of advertising compared to internet users in western countries. Ad blocking software and plugins have been, so far, more common in the West than in China where banner advertising is still growing.

Also, the type of banners ads that are considered to be more effective in China tend to be flashier and more animated, something that Western users typically find most annoying.

According to March 2016 polling by iResearch China, the ad's relevancy is the most important factor in user's decision to click it (36.5% indicated that as the main factor), followed by the quality of the copy (34%).

32.5% of respondents indicated that promotional info, such as discounts, coupons or attractive pricing prompted their clicks. Finally, great visuals and sound effects is what attracts 31.4% of people.

Much less visitors were clicking an ad based on frequency – only 15.3% clicked an ad because they have seen it multiple times. However, that is still a fairly high number that makes retargeting (remarketing) a highly effective strategy for serving banner ads in China.

Let's have a closer look at different types of banner ads in China and their effectiveness.

Banners on ecommerce sites

According to various data, banner ads on Chinese ecommerce sites are, by far, the most effective. According to iResearch, nearly 8 in 10 users paid attention to those ads and over 60% of users routinely click them. Since such advertising is often highly relevant to users who are searching for specific products, those results are not surprising.

Banners on portals and search engines

Over 70% would notice ads on portals and search engines and over half would click them which makes those site the next best channel after ecommerce sites for placing banners ads. Such high numbers are explained by the fact that there is a higher degree of intent and interest on the part of people who are searching for a specific term or visit specialized websites.

Banners on video sites

Although about 70% of visitors to video sites like Youku or PPTV notice the ads, they are the most disliked types of banners ads. Another research from Tencent Penguin Intelligence found that the majority of internet users aged between 16 and 20 did not watch video ads, and 11.6% even said that they were "intolerable." These types of ads are mostly disliked on mobile. With the typical length of a pre-roll ad on Youku being about 1 minute, those finding are hardly surprising.

Banners on social media sites

In general, banner advertising on social media sites such as Weibo is often considered ineffective. Another research by Kantar, discovered that a dismal 13% of visitors on those sites liked such ads while 24.2% said they were put off by them and 42.1% simply ignored them altogether. In my experience, post boosts work much better in social media due to their higher relevancy to users' interests.

Mobile banner ads

Mobile ads is the fastest growing sector which offers the most potential. New mobile ads networks are improving efficiency, although the industry is still in the experimentation stage. Many networks are still looking for the best ways to monetize and the prices may vary widely. One of the biggest problems with mobile ads is the fact that they often get clicked by accident. This, in part, is caused by limited "real estate" of the small mobile phone screens. On the other hand, larger smartphones and "phablets" offer more potential.

Ads on gaming sites

The biggest problem with these type of banner ads in China is the relevancy – it is hard to figure out precisely who would be interested in checking out the latest fast food restaurant offer while playing a game. Even though the marketing reach with gaming ads can be quite large, CTR is often low. Most effective banner ads on gaming sites and mobile games often feature new games and related apps installs rather than unrelated or broad subjects.

Conclusion

There is no question that ignoring the second largest, and one of the most dynamic consumer markets in the world is not an option for any business with global aspirations. However, simple copying and pasting of the strategies from familiar markets to China is unlikely to be an effective approach.

The main rationale behind developing a separate strategy for Chinese market is the fact that China is, in many ways, a unique case. First of all, the largest and most influential digital advertisers, such as Facebook and Google, were kept out of the market long enough for new ecosystem, with its own technology and methods, to take hold.

The second reason is that Chinese market is just too vast to be able to dictate its own rules of the game. Foreign businesses have no choice but to adapt if they stand any chance to succeed and compete successfully.

Finally, the extremely fast pace of consumer market growth and homegrown technological development enabled China to skip several steps that Western markets went through in the past. This different route has significantly altered the present situation and continues affecting the way things are progressing at present. The examples include the advanced state of online and mobile payments, increasingly mobile nature of online interactions and enormous ecommerce component.

I hope that this summary of marketing methods for Chinese market has given you better perspective on what could be applicable for your business to achieve your goals.

Useful resources

- For new updates on marketing in China, make sure to visit to my blog at sampi.co/blog and sign up for my weekly newsletter.

- Another great way to stay informed is connecting with me on Twitter @sampimarketing.

- Join discussion on this Facebook page dedicated to news about business and marketing in China: www.facebook.com/sampimarketing/

- I regularly share new presentations that cover various aspects of marketing in China at slideshare.net/sampimarketing

- If you are looking for technical stuff, Technode.com is the Asian equivalent of TechCrunch that delivers great news of the latest technology used in China marketing.

- More analytical data and stats can be found in chinainternetwatch.com (paid subscription is required for premium content).

- ThoughtfulChina is the best China business and marketing channel on YouTube: https://www.youtube.com/user/ThoughtfulChina

- Chinalawblog.com is the excellent source of information on various legal aspects of doing business in China.

19189061R00106

Printed in Poland
by Amazon Fulfillment
Poland Sp. z o.o., Wrocław